I0415115

ECONOMIC SUICIDE!

14 FEBRUARY 2011, GOVERNMENT SPENDING CUTS UPDATE:

Like I've said many times before, less than five percent of the USA population truly understands how an economy really works and that includes learned economists. They don't teach what I tell you in schools.

This nation has took the course of least resistance and allowed the liberals to create this monster size welfare state beast that has all but completely destroyed our once strong nuclear and extended family system.

Common sense should tell anyone that understands basic economics that mass government spending cuts at once are going to speed up the collapse of this welfare state by creating hoards of new dependents and mouths to feed.

What is truly needed is a back to survival basics, meaning a way must be found to rebuild the nations nuclear and extended family system and get back to a true free market place economy or as near as possible. But, that can never be done with government taxing the hell out of businesses to kingdom come.

I understand, but less than five percent of the general population understands that all profit originates with some type of trade or business transaction from the private sector. And the sad fact is the heavy hand of government taxes and self-initiative killing regulations is drying up that profit generating well. And guess what? Government will dry up, too.

The only way this great nation is going to be saved is through private enterprise. Government must be voted back to its designated role in our free republic as the guardian and protector and doing only what the people can't do for themselves.

A nation cannot remain free and survive with government in the role of super family provider simply because without a survival need the two family household will soon disappear and so will the nation.

As a man of great supernatural wisdom I suggest we start the process by first completely eliminating the minimum wage and government must stop giving anyone free money on an individual basis. That doesn't include anyone working for government.

The government should help the poor and

unemployed by establishing government run commissaries, houses, and clinics with the use of token only to qualify, then the free market will remain free not contaminated and inflated out of sight like it is now.

Otherwise, in a welfare state any drastic government spending cuts is only going to mean a smaller pie to be shared by many more dependents and mouths to feed. Jesus wept.

My God! I slam my hat on the floor! Lord help us! It is sad and hard for me to watch my beloved homeland commit economic suicide! For several years I have been ranting and raving at the top of my voice but it is like water off a ducks back, no one will listen and I'm totally ignored, what else one can do.

This nation is on an unsustainable course leading to sure doom. But, what do we do? The conservatives are fixing to jump out of the hot water into the fire. As I watch this so called conservative government spending cut craze go on as if it is some kind of fascinating game being played.

Sure, this nation is headed toward doom and something definite need to be done but in my view economic suicide is not the answer. Opinions are like a-holes with everyone having one including me. Just because someone is a learned economist doesn't mean he/she truly knows what the hell is going on.

You keep believing the egg heads with their always toeing the government line with figures to support it and we all are gonna perish. Don't believe anything just because I say it, but also don't dismiss anything I say when it is based on over 5000 years of tried and true civilization proof.

When I pound and pound away on the necessity of the nuclear and extended family system and the fact that a genuine free market place economy has never failed to produce an over abundance of everything you can stake your life on it.

No system of government has ever survived in the history of mankind without the nuclear family unit head of household filling the role as the provider. That last statement lead to this truth which I believe is the root cause of America's economic and culture meltdown. And until this root cause is dealt with and corrected this nation will never survive as a free nation.

The root cause I'm referring to started with the "New deal" when the liberals seized the nuclear family provider role from the traditional male head of household and then government became a sugar daddy.

That one act did something to the African American race that even slavery couldn't do. That root cause has almost completely destroyed the once proud and safe all black neighbor hoods. It has almost completely destroyed the once strong black nuclear and extended family system and community.

Proportional wise more African Americans babies are killed in the wombs than anywhere on earth. Also, approaching 80 percent of all African Americans babies are born out of wedlock.

Now, what do all of that have to do with America's economic problems? A lot, once government became a super sugar daddy family provider (and it is a sugar daddy provider because it has never enforced discipline or demanded qualification to receive free handouts) it has not only destroyed our economy it has rotted away our culture, too.

For all of these years conservatives have stood by and let the liberals grow this vast welfare state into a super beast. Now over 95 percent of the population expects government to always be there to take care of them if they need it.

So, I think it is wrong for conservatives to snatch that false sense of hope from under these people without throwing them some kind of a lifeline. I believe less than five percent of the population understand basic economic because all of these people think cutting government spending is going to reduce the size of government, wrong.

It is going to increase the size of government by increasing the government dole population. The only way to reduce big government when it is a welfare state is to reduce government's role as a family provider.

I have offered a great **suggestion** (www.FLSirmans.com/NoMinimumWageTest) on how to solve the dilemma, because with a welfare state the more you cut government spending the more you put people out of work and increase government dependency.

Also, increasing the government's dependency population forces government to raise taxes even more on the businesses left standing thereby driving even more people out of work. Government should never give out free money on an individual basis.

Government should help the poor and unemployed by establishing temporary government run commissaries, housing, and clinics with the use of tokens only to qualify. Government should never give free money and food stamps to anyone on an individual basis because that is what has destroyed our economy.

Government giving out free money on an individual basis destroys the balance between the merchant and the consumer. So, when government gives the poor the money to pay the merchants higher and higher prices that allows the merchants to stay in business and keep prices high for everyone.

Then government raises taxes higher and higher on the merchants to provide care for more and more government dependents in a never ending upward spiral. Lord save this great nation.

SIRMANS LOG: 10 FEBRUARY 2011, 2305 HOURS.

LIBERALS DARE CONSERVATIVES TO MAKE THEIR DAY, DO MASSIVE

SPENDING CUTS!

01 FEBRUARY 2011, 0925 HOURS: UPDATE

The main reason I'm so against conservatives doing massive government spending cuts out of the blue is because the liberals with their welfare state has severely crippled private enterprise and nearly destroyed the once strong reliable nuclear and extended family system in this nation.

Before the "New deal" came along the people's survival depended on private enterprise and the strong reliable nuclear and extended family system and hardly anyone depended on government for their survival.

Balance is the key, social security was a good thing as a supplement for the handicapped, widows, and the elderly but everyone knows that balance is no longer the case.

Now, the liberals with their welfare state have created masses upon masses of government dependents and have all but destroyed our once strong nuclear and extended family system umbrella.

So, in my eyes it would be cruel and unfair for conservatives to snatch the rug from under these people before throwing them some type of lifeline.

The lifeline I have suggested is to stop all government free money handouts to anyone on an individual basis because that destroys the free market place and is what keeps driving prices higher and higher for everyone.

Once that is done establish temporary government commissaries, houses, and clinics that will require tokens only to participate, that way the national currency and the free market will stay pure and won't be contaminated with uncontrolled inflation.

So, I say give these people a lifeline first, next eliminate the minimum wage, then conservatives "Do your thing" cut taxes, spending and everything else to the bone, hurrah, hurrah...

30 JANUARY 2011, 1855 HOURS: UPDATE

I'm confused! I'm hearing that cutting government spending is going to increase jobs. I say poppy cock, hogwash, bull, nonsense; I beg your difference because I'm convinced that when you cut government spending you put people out of work.

There is no way of getting around that fact. Now, if you tell me you are cutting taxes then I agree that is going to increase jobs, but government spending, no way. If you do massive cuts in government spending that is going to put massive amounts of people out of work.

The question is what is going to happen to these people? Do these people find new jobs or do they greatly increase the government dole population. Obvious the dole population is going to increase because hardly anyone can find a job as it is.

If conservatives actually believe that massive cuts in government spending are going to increase jobs, then we are in more trouble than even I could imagine. Who am I, but I must say unless somebody start taking me serious and listening to some of my ideas this run-a-way economic train is definite going to crash and burn.

I'm not totally against cuts in government spending, but you can't ignore the facts. When you cut government entitlements that cuts their administrative staff and if it includes less money going to recipients, too, anyway you look at it, that is money that won't be available to retailers.

As long as more than forty percent of the American people depend on the government as their super provider they will never vote to bite the hand that feeds them.

So, anything conservatives do that don't work to take back the provider role for the individual family unit where it had been for over 5,000 years until the "New deal" came along is a waste of time.

MY Warning to the Tea party and conservatives, if you do massive government cuts in spending its going to backfire on you. The first thing is it won't stop job loss or truly control government spending it will only be committing political suicide.

Remember, the unemployment rate is already extremely high and massive government cuts all at once is going to mean even more massive unemployment. Sure, something can be done but that ain't the way to go about it.

Conservatives must get all of their ducks in a row first; I will get to my suggested way to go about it later. If the conservative insist on plowing ahead with massive cut in government spending all it is going to do is put the liberals back in power.

They are the ones that overall caused the fix we are in today starting with the "New deal." Again you will almost never hear me mentioning a political party simply because there are a lot of under cover liberals in the Republican Party and almost vice versa in the Democratic Party.

I often refer to liberals as being shallow but you won't ever hear me referring to liberals as being dumb or stupid. Overall liberals are much smarter and intelligent than conservatives in my view, why do you think they were able to take over almost all of our colleges and universities and most of the institutions in this country.

But, in my view they are still shallow surface dweller that should never control the long term destiny of a country. Once the "New deal" gave them the excuse to seize the social and family provider role for themselves they have never looked back, they kept almost absolute power for forty years.

They did it simply by giving the people what the people wanted at taxpayer's expense, which they are still doing to this day. And I don't think they know or care if that destroys character in the people and will bankrupt the country; I believe they feel to hell with country as long as it keeps them in power.

Anyone with an ounce of common sense knows to keep overspending like the government is doing is going to destroy this great nation. Still, do you know anyone with an ounce of common sense that believes with liberal in power they will ever control overspending, I don't.

So, it's very simple, if this great nation is ever going to be saved, the conservative will have to fight against all odds to do it. Saving this great nation is something a lot easier said than done because the shallow minded liberals have not only destroyed the economy they have created masses of dependent voter with a flawed do-for-me mentality.

If conservatives are going to save this great country it can't be done by taking away the only means the masses of government dependents has been conditioned to survive on without some guaranteed replacement.

That is why if the conservatives go ahead with massive government cut in spending its going to put many more out of work, and I will guarantee you they will be voted out of office even with people knowing something must be done about overspending.

Again, I will promise you as long as government is in its all powerful role of social and family provider, government over spending will never be brought under control, the politics will never allow it because the liberals will see you in hell first before they will ever stop growing government.

I have already given the best conservative solution that I know of in the form of a suggestion. My suggestion is to **first run a test** (www.FLSirmans.com/NoMinimumWageTest) in a large northeastern city to test the theory and work out any kinks.

The purpose of the suggestion is to stop government from giving out free money on an individual basis. That will stop government from subsidizing higher and higher prices thereby allowing poor people to pay their own health cost and other living cost.

I know most people will think my suggestion is not a good solution but it is. The main reason is the people dependent on the government to survive must know that they will not be abandoned with any food, shelter, warmth, or medical care.

That is what I meant by conservatives having

all of their ducks in a row, conservatives must never do massive government spending cut before guaranteeing the poor and the unemployed a means to survive, But, they should never give out free money on an individual basis if the free market economy is to survive.

The poor and unemployed should be given token that can only be spent in temporary government run commissaries, housing, kitchen, and clinics. Then with government no longer giving out free money on an individual basis prices will have to drop to where the poor can pay for their own medical care and other cost or no merchants can stay in business.

I don't see any other way to political get past the liberals and save this great country's economy from crashing and burning. Temporary running government run commissaries, housing, kitchens, and clinics will cost money but that type of spending doesn't destroy the free market place and drive up consumer prices for everyone like what's happening now.

Then if the minimum wage is eliminated the economy can't help but boom. Sure, at first the liberals and the masses of government dependents will never accept something like this and there will be an outrageous outcry.

But, with a little time the majority population will come around, because it knows we definitely are on a course to doom. Even the conservatives might not be on board for this, but I have made my case.

Now, it is up to others to take it from here, I will guarantee you, you will never defeat the liberals with cold turkey massive government spending cuts, that is only going to get conservatives kicked out of office.
.
No one has to take my advice for anything just continue on your merry way, we'll see.
SIRMANS LOG: 27 JANUARY 2011, 0016 HOURS.

JOBS, THAT ELUSIVE CREATURE GOVERNMENT IS TRYING TO FIND!
20 JANUARY 2011, 1144 HOURS.
JUST AN OBSERVATION:
On TV I see all of the pundits and talking heads from the left and the right trying to figure out Sarah Palin and why she is such a lighting rod.

They watch and weigh every word she speaks trying to find a clue to as to what makes her tick. The liberals are almost out of their minds with frustration, anger, and a host of other emotions, all for reasons they themselves can't give a logical reason for.

To me the core reason is very simple and very clear. I'll just cut through the chase and quickly give you the core reason. The core reason is not political. The core reason and drive behind all of this fuss is the liberal instinct.

.

The liberals by instinct see her as a deadly moral threat, especially liberal women and to their progress. The liberals are in boot shaking fear that she will get some real power, but they will never admit that, they just keep say she don't have a snowball chance in hell of winning.

.

Most conservatives and other are mostly fascinated by the whole thing and can't understand why the liberals dislike her so much. Some people are for her only because the liberals hate her so much.

Ever since the "New deal" moral and spiritual values in the USA has been declining and is now to the point that liberals will stop at nothing to try to destroy any genuine high moral person in the political arena. And they are right to be fearful because their forty years of absolute rule or to rule at all in the future is going to become more and more remote.

That is because the once big three no longer has absolute control over all free speech news, thanks to the blogs, talk radio, and other alternatives.
.
Now the real truth is getting through to educate the people on the dire fix the liberals have put this great nation in. That is my one man analysis on what is taking place with Governor Palin.
.
However, the liberals can never be counted out or taken for granted because they do have one powerful advantage over genuine conservatives. Hardcore liberal lions will stop at nothing to have their way providing they can legal get away with it.
.
Whereas, most hardcore genuine conservatives has moral and self-restraint boundaries. Most genuine conservatives are bound by self-respect for the truth, for the protection of unborn future generations, and other moral considerations that would never deter a die-hard liberal from delivering a knock out punch.
.
These people are almost unstoppable in obtaining their goals. The only thing that is

going to stop the liberals and save this great nation from total doom is to educate the majority public. Otherwise the liberals are too shallow to recognize their sure path to self-destruction to themselves and to the nation.

18 JANUARY 2011, 1730 HOURS
JUST AN OBSERVATION:

If you sit down to a card game and stake someone to bet against you then you end up owing them a lot of money how dumb is that. Well, this really happened to our drunk on spending welfare state, unbelievable. Boo hoo, cry me a river.

UPDATE: 16 JANUARY 2011, 0850 HOURS.
SOUL SEARCHING OUT LOUD!

Why! Why! Oh Lord, why do I continue on with this, where do this drive come from to continue on writing. I'm not selling enough books to enrich myself; this is almost a curse to me, why! Why! Why...

I'm no fool I know 98 percent of the people disagrees with my views, especially completely eliminating the minimum wage. Still, for some reason beyond me I'm driven by some unknown energy or destiny to plod on.

Just maybe I can do even a small thing to aid in keeping millions upon millions from starving to death when this economy crash and burn. There are no guarantees in life and I know my views may be wrong.

But still, it is insane for this great nation to continue on a course that every wise man/woman knows can't be sustained. Even a fool knows you must try to stop a run away train (The economy) even if you fail, I only see more money printing and government spending.

Sometimes under extreme conditions requires extreme actions and I don't see that happening. I suggested a testing of the **"No minimum wage"** (www.FLSirmans.com/NoMinimumWageTest) in practice in a large northeastern city, mute was the answer.

I don't care what it takes this run away train economy must be stopped before it crashes and burns with possible 100 million people starving to death afterward, and they won't even run a simple little **test** that may show how to save millions of lives., shame on you welfare state and egg heads. I take a moment of silence, you think about it.

CURRENT EVENT OPINION: 16 JANUARY 2011, 0855 HOURS.
I SIT NEXT TO YOU, YOU SIT NEXT TO ME!

Hogwash! It never ceases to amaze me of the bold scheming of the liberal mind. Now, all of a sudden liberals want to get rid of all labels and sit next to the opposition.

Why now? Do anyone think they would have come up with this before the last election, I don't. I think all of this new good intention is just a tactic to confuse the public. Right now they know the liberal ticket is not the hottest ticket in town so why not hid in plain sight.

Sure, if this is a genuine goodwill effort to last over time no matter who is on top I'm all for it but I don't think that is the case. Please don't hate on me, I'm only one man with one view and I could be wrong.

CURRENT EVENT COMMENT: 12 JANUARY 2011, 2016 HOURS.
FREE SPEECH:

Everyone agrees that unnecessarily shouting fire in an open theater must be banned. But, going past something simple like that could come to no ending.

It could lead to being punished for coughing at the wrong time in the wrong place. No one can predict where it will all end if we go down this political correctness road. Liberals are not against free speech, they are just against speech that is not shallow and irresponsible like their own.

They are too shallow to understand that there is a much bigger world out there than their shallowness can see. Over a hundred years or so ago the only place you could find a liberal was from a rich family and maybe on a college campus.

Today, around eighty years after the "New deal" they are crawling out of the wood works and everywhere, they have completely taken over our great colleges and universities. I tip my hat to them, these are awesome people there is nothing they will not do to attain their goals.

With 20 percent or less of the total population these good intention shallow super aggressive people for all practical purpose has taken over and spent and ran this great country into the ground since the "New deal."

They grabbed this awesome power by taking

the course of least resistance and handing out free government goodies at tax payer's expense.

That is something that plays to our very basic human instincts and its extremely hard for almost everyone to resist the easy life of government assured pleasure and comfort. But, now we are face to face with that age old axiom, "There are no free rides in nature," someone always pays one way or another and it may be in blood, sweat, or tears.

Only now with the once big three no longer in complete monopoly like control of all free speech news has the vise like liberal death grip on this nation's throat begun to loosen.

Now real true free speech is finally getting through to the people, I can only hope it's not too late to save this great nation from economic collapse and total liberal destruction. Amen, praise be to God.

UPDATE: 10 JANUARY 2011, 1200 HOURS.

I'm not against government spending to help people in severe need, but, what I am against is the type of government spending since the "New deal" that have destroyed our economy, culture, and nation almost to the point of no return.

I don't have a problem with the government spending like crazy as long as it doesn't hand out money on an individual basis. Handing out money on an individual basis destroys the natural balance between the buyer and the seller or the merchant and the consumer that in turn ignites the inflationary spiraling that is causing this insane runaway economy we have today.

Government giving out money on an individual basis is like cancer it first attacks and destroys the free market place economy, then the nation's culture, and on and on until a hollered out shell of a nation is left.

I don't enjoy being a spoil sport, party pooper; raining on anybody's parade, or any other bad news metaphor. But, one thing about me is no matter what it is I'm going to face it head on.

I have faced dreadful almost unbearable things all of my life and found you always come out better in the end no matter the results. Even if you are wrong face your mistake and try again.

I don't think this nation's leadership is willing

to truly face down the dire situation our economy and nation are in. And I think this great nation will be left unprepared when the bottom falls out which anyone with an ounce of economic sense know is going to happen.

UPDATE: 10 JANUARY 2011, 0813 HOURS.

Okay, okay if my "No minimum wage" is so insane and unworkable why not at the least run a test case and see what happens. After all I'm talking about the future survival of this great nation and we are a civilized people, who can be against running a test.

Why not select Detroit or any large northeastern city for a five year "No minimum wage" test case and see what happens in practice. I suggest First grandfather clause in all existing conditions. But, once the test takes effect I suggest no new government cash be given out on an individual basis.

I suggest some of the acres and acres of vacant building be used as government run commissaries, clinics or whatever is needed on a community wise basis. I believe this nation need to start preparing no matter how small on what I and all wise men/women know is coming soon to this great nation.

JOBS, THAT ELUSIVE CREATURE GOVERNMENT IS TRYING TO FIND!

As a self-made writer, publisher, philosopher, inventor, and original creative thinker, I decided to weigh in here on the lack of jobs debacle.

The first misconception is the purpose of a business or to go into business is to provide jobs. The need and reason for a business is to enrich or create a profit for the owner or owners and providing jobs is only a byproduct.

That being the case government goal and aim should be to set policies that will allow businesses to make more profit not less. And at the very least not create mountains of red tape. Nature's supreme law of "Natural selection" that controls everything on earth is base solely on a "Survival need."

For anything to survive or exist any period of time there must be a "Survival need" for it to exist or it will crease to exist, and that includes jobs. It is very simple if a business truly need more help or job seekers it will hire them, their main complaint or problem is finding qualified job seekers.

26

The main reason government is desperate in job promoting is all of the dependents the welfare state has created since the "New deal" is coming with pitch forks if the provider checks isn't delivered. Now I refer back to the broken record that I have been playing for many years.

The ultimatum is either we give up feeding the welfare state beast or the great USA perishes. There is no other way out, the financial burdens and cost is simply going to kill this economy.

I believe the government as a social and family provider since the "New deal' has grown into this financial beast that is impossible to feed, and it is now eating the great USA out of a house and home.

To not face this reality is insane, stupid, and beyond irresponsible, it is sheer madness. With my supernatural wisdom I have suggested a means to defuse this time bomb from causing a total collapsing of the world's global economy, but to no avail, I'm totally ignored and dismissed as a nut case.

Maybe millions upon millions live could be saved, but what can I say, I'm seen as just a nobody trying play on the world's stage. I believe and suggested that completely eliminating the minimum wage would provide a way back to sanity and slowly slow down this runaway welfare state economy, stop it and reverse back away from the cliff it is about to go over.

Then with over 5000 years of proven human survival evolution we can head in the direction of the strong nuclear and extended family system. That will allow the one breadwinner household to rebound and again lead to unsurpassed greatness for the land of the free and home of the brave.

What? Well, I'm waiting! I'm waiting for the egg heads to say how they are going to stop this runaway economy from going over the cliff to crash and burn! I'm waiting for anyone to offer a better solution than mine! Will some mature adult please step up!

I know no liberal is going to step up they are too shallow to see any survival threat until it is tearing down the front door. Sure, ultimately all survival is based on need, but, the bonus to life is what do we want and desire which can be manipulated.

So, a business may not need more employees but if it is going to lead to enough profit to make it worthwhile then greed will kick in. There is no greater motivating energy force on earth than greed.

Greed is the only force that can make a free people and a free market place produce more of everything than any one nation can use. And are the main reason communist government, socialist government, and any system that shuts down greed will fail unless there are abundance natural resources to sell.

Greed is like electricity very dangerous but when harnessed is the most powerful motivating energy force on earth. If the USA government truly wants to produce more jobs it first must eliminate mountains of red tape greatly relieve the tax bite to allow businesses to make enough profit to make growth worth the effort.

That and that alone will free up entrepreneurs then greed will take it from there and boom the economy. But, the real solution in the end must be to get the welfare state out of the social and family provider role it is now playing.
SIRMANS LOG: 8 JANUARY 2011, 1216 HOURS.

<u>WELFARE STATE BEAST MUST BE STARVED OUT OF THE PROVIDER</u>

ROLE!
BRIEF UPDATE:

When government gives out money on an individual basis to the poor in the long run it is not helping the poor or the country.

What that is doing is destroying the free market place which in time will hurt everyone and hurt the poor the most by driving the cost of living out of sight.

If the government truly wants to help the poor without doing a lot of damage and in the end destroy the country, it should establish government Commissaries, government housing, government clinic, or even issue government token chips.

Doing it that way wouldn't destroy the free market place like government has been doing ever since the "New deal." Issuing food stamps is a no, no because that is technical the same as giving out money on an individual basis.

Government can spend like hell all it wants to as long as it doesn't give out money on an individual basis because that is the one thing that affects and destroys the free market place.

In a natural healthy economy there is a natural balance between the merchant and the consumer that keeps the cost of living affordable and under control. But, when government gets involve it is like someone putting his thumb on the scale.

There is no way a greedy merchant can decide to charge a higher price than his competition and stay in business without government involvement because not enough people already have the money.

Cry me a river, and the government thinks it is helping the poor by handing out money on an individual basis. So, even now as back then the egg heads ignore and dismisses everything someone like me may say, even if it makes totally good sense and is sound judgment.

Like I've said thousands of times the economy is just one leg of the four leg survival stool, as a supposition if the USA had all of the money it needed to spend on anything it wanted to it still wouldn't save us from total doom, because the welfare state has rotted away the core of this great nation, there is legal murder in the womb and sodomy is no longer a kept secret in the military.

Sodomy the same as abortion on demand are instinctually a threat to future survival in almost all cases. Understanding this fact is something that can't be taught, but anyone one with a strong survival instinct will automatic knows this without being told.

Remember, I don't make any rules I just happen to have a super strong survival instinct that recognizes inherent threats to survival, no matter what they are.
LAST ENTRY: 22 DECEMBER 2010, 0305 HOURS.

WELFARE STATE BEAST MUST BE STARVED OUT OF THE PROVIDER ROLE!
Hear ye! Hear ye! Hear ye! To any one within the range of my voice, unlike the liberals hiding their real intentions, my intentions are to try to drive the welfare state out of being an individual family unit provider.

I don't believe there is anyway this great nation can survive and be saved as long as our super welfare state beast is in the family provider role it now plays.

I think the family provider role should be returned back to the individual family unit, and government should stay with protecting and defending the nation and doing only that which the people can't do for themselves.

Our super welfare state beast has destroyed our culture to the point that we are living in the now, me first, what do I get out of it, I want mine, I want it all, screw future generations, It's just a fetus, gimmy, gimmy, and on and on.

Self-sacrificing for the long term good of the country and sometimes willingly giving up a right for wrong for the long term good of the country is almost unheard of with most of today's leadership.

I just want everyone to know that I think the destruction of our nuclear and extended family system was caused by our liberal induced welfare state, and it have placed this great nation at deaths door.

I blame almost all of it on our liberal induced welfare state starting with the "New deal." Their intent was not to destroy the country, their intent was to irresponsible grab power and keep it at all cost by handing out free goodies at tax payers expense.

Sure, during hard and trying times the government has a responsibility to provide on temporary basis community wise only emergency kitchens, shelters, and clinics, anything more will in time take away the need for the nuclear and extended family system thereby destroying the nuclear and extended family system, which have happen in the USA.

The individual family provider role must remain in the hands of the individual family unit breadwinner for any nation or society to survive long term.

We as a nation have failed to safeguard our nuclear family unit which is nature's first law of human survival enforced by its supreme law of "Natural selection." There has never been a surviving society in the history of mankind without the nuclear family unit.

The process of "natural selection is chasing this nation down and closing in on us and we are gonna pay dearly for destroying our nuclear and extended family system, hopefully we will survive as a nation.

About me: It may be as much as 95 percent of the people will see me as a cold and uncaring monster, but, when the bottom falls out of this welfare state and we won't have a leg to stand on , I will be the hero, by then it may be too late.

I'm all about doing the greater good meaning

the long term survival of the entire species, not just short term pleasure and comfort, especially to those that don't do anything to earn their keep. I'm human I have feeling the same as all people.

I take no pleasure in being disliked and frowned upon, but, I believe I have been chosen by destiny to help save this great nation and I cannot and will not dialect my duty come hell or high waters. Long live the great USA.

When I say get rid of the minimum wage the first thing most people will think is, my God! And think businesses will be in a race to see who can pay the least amount in wages. The truth is no one knows because it is a natural selection process and a business still has to pay the best wages to get the best people.

Plus, that is only one side of the coin, the other side of the coin is no business can charge more than the poor can afford to pay and stay in business, that is unless the government gives the poor the money to pay whatever price a business may charge.

Getting rid of the minimum wage would severely limit governments ability to drive up prices for everyone when it pays the poor enough money to keep high priced merchants in business, otherwise the cost of living could never out distance what the poor man could afford. Right now the cost of living is far above what a one breadwinner provider can afford.

The merchant has to charge higher and higher prices to pay higher and higher taxes, license fees, permit fees, and countless other government mandates even before any business profit is made. And the government keeps growing bigger and bigger needing even more taxes to be even a bigger sugar daddy in a no ending inflationary spiral. Even a moron should see the hand writing on the wall, but oh no, not a shallow minded liberal.

It is impossible for this system not to crash no matter what the egg heads say. While all of this has been going on since the "New deal" it has hollered out the foundation and culture core of this great nation and left us with no means to survive through hard times or a severe crisis.

SIRMANS LOG: 18 DECEMBER 2010, 0204 HOURS.

DETROIT IS A LIBERAL EXAMPLE THAT AWAITS US ALL!!!
There was never a minimum wage before the "New deal" and this nation have been around

well over 200 years
I love liberals some of my best friends are
liberals we all are human beings, some of us
are very shallow and some of us has great
depth.

More than anyone else the liberals complains
about no jobs, kids don't have enough to eat,
and on and on. But, they are shallow and
don't have the depth to realize that
practically all of these ills are the direct
result of their liberal policies more than
anyone Else's.

I just shake my head and realize these
liberals are like spoiled kids; you can't dislike
them for their shallowness. I'm more
saddened than hostile at them, but, this is
not Child's play this is the real world that is
being screwed up.

This is why I try so hard to educate people
with my deep wisdom and sound judgment.
Actually our whole society is at fault for
being seduced and lulled so far astray from
what reasonable men and women know is
down the wrong path.

It is natural for everything in nature to take
the course of least resistance including man,
but, we are human beings with the ability to
reason and we should know better.

We should know that the road down the course of least resistance leads to "Easy come easy go." We should know that the road down the gambling path leads to a "Something for nothing mentality."

We should know that any road leading away from a strong nuclear and extended family system leads to murder in the womb and leaving our young undisciplined and unprepared for survival. We should know that good times are not going to last forever.

This liberal created welfare state has just about destroyed our nuclear and extended family system, our once super strong religious and moral values, and any capacity to barter with many, many small farmers and home gardeners, we have in a sense ate our seed corn and drink our priming water.

Now, we have almost nothing in terms of surviving through hard times, I pity the fool. By putting all of our eggs and faith in one super welfare state beast we are almost done in terms of emergency survival.

Look at what the liberals has done to the once great motor city and practical all of the big northeastern cities. The liberals have run these cities almost totally unopposed for years and look at the result, but, they are still blaming everybody else and his brother.

Liberal policies have driven away businesses, the middle class, and everyone else with the means to escape. With sensible policies Detroit city can be saved with all of those abandon building coming alive and booming. All it takes is getting rid of the national minimum wage.

The egg heads think I'm stupid and they are the one's that know it all. I say eliminating the minimum wage is our only hope. It is true no matter if nobody believes it but me. As long as I have the mean I will keep pounding and shouting to anyone who will listen to my drumbeat of junking the minimum wage.

I don't think it will but I know it could turn our whole economy upside down. The fact is we don't really have a choice if we want to survive as a nation, otherwise we will end up as a region in some world body.

Anyone with an ounce of economic sense knows the current system we have is going to collapse, no one knows the day and hour, but they know it's going to happen. They are in denial and will never admit it in public but I will and continue to do so, unless they shut me down.

I know I'm branded and seen as a nut case, so be it, I'm only writing what I truly believe, I don't know why I'm doing this, I feel it must be destiny, sometimes I feel like a driven man on a treadmill and can't get off. In fact I hate the limelight and am uncomfortable around most people, especially strangers.

If the minimum wage is gotten rid of there is nothing saying that businesses will pay lower wages. A true free market place which it would be without any forced wages up or down. That would create a natural balance.

Sure, the cost of living would have to come down but I don't believe it would drop like a rock. Very few people would work for a dollar an hour because you couldn't buy enough to make it worth while.

But, in time the cost of living and the buying power of the dollar would seek a reasonable balance, whereas right now the average salary is far too low to come close to meeting the cost of living. The cost of living would seek a level down where one head of household could provide for a whole family.

Everything including medical cost would seek

a natural level down to where everyone could pay out of pocket. If a business wanted the best workers it would still have to pay the best wages.

Sure, I keep harping on getting rid of the minimum wage, but the truth is if we don't do it the whole system is going to collapse and millions upon millions are going to stave to death.

You don't have to believe me, just keep feeding our liberal welfare state beast and we'll all find out sooner than we think.

.

I believe anything that will starve the beast out of its all powerful social and family provider role is a good thing and the only way to save the United States of America. Unlike the liberals I will never hide my true beliefs.

SIRMANS LOG: 14 DECEMBER 2010, 0021 HOURS

THE IGNORANCE OF ATTACKING THE RICH!

I feel a need to weigh in again on this subject. I believe anybody that attacks the rich is ignorant on what makes a democracy work or is just no friend of freedom and democracy.

Attacking the rich is the first thing a future dictator will do because he knows the rich is the life blood that makes a democracy works. There has never been and never will be a rich and prosperous country without a lot of rich people to bring it about.

Rich people are not the same as poor people with money, there is a world of difference in motivation and attitude. As a supposition if all of the money in this country were spread equally among the people, it wouldn't take but a few years for almost all of the money to be back in the same hands.

Entrepreneur's registers very high in altruism which is especially true when rewarded properly. Now, at the very opposite end of the totem pole where you will find the most dead beats and cop-out losers, and if you just scratch a little below the surface you will almost always find a very selfish self-centered individual.

Any type of government or economic system that won't let a lot of people become rich is going to fail, unless it is blessed with a lot of natural resources. These liberals and masses of government dependents don't have a clue as to what truly made this country great.

Throughout all of the early struggles this nation's culture always remained intact until the "New deal" came along. That is when the Liberals seized the traditional nuclear family provider role for themselves, and it wasn't long after that the black man was completely kicked out of the house.

Since then the liberals has slowly created social program after social program that conditions masses upon masses of people not to feel personally responsible for their own survival. These people have come to believe that it always someone else's responsibility or fault for their survival.

What are they going to do when this government is broke and can't borrow any more money or continue printing so much phony money that our currency will soon have the same worth as monopoly money?

Now the liberals are going all out attacking the rich instead of being thankful for the rich that supplies them with a job which dead beats will never do. What you see on the surface and out front is never what it really takes to be a super achiever.

That is just a fraction of what it takes, you don't know it, but while you are in your easy chair or recliner kicked back with a beer or watching your favorite movie or TV program, the super achievers are doing backbreaking work or toiling away 15, 16, or more hour's a day.

With very few exceptions rich and successful people truly work hard and earn the money they make. Meanwhile the welfare state and its hoard of government dependents think they have a right to take that money hand some back and spend the rest as they please.

Then they act like they are doing the rich and super achievers a favor by giving them back some of their own money. The fact is not the rich nor is anyone actually getting a tax cut it is just staying at the same rate it's been for the last ten years.

If the liberals and big spenders had the power they would without a doubt spend this country into total oblivion and regress us all back to the Stone Age. Then while dragging the women by their hair into caves they would still be yelling it's the republicans fault.

Like I have said many times before, when you create a situation where the rich can no longer keep or hold on to their money that is the beginning to the end of freedom and democracy. The rich is the glue that holds every democracy together.

Like a broken record I repeat, as long as government is in the role of super family provider that is the force and drive that propels it to stop at nothing to retain that power that includes everything it can beg, borrow, and steal, to keep their God like power.

Government will never go back to just protecting the country both internally and externally and doing only what the people can't do for themselves. Anyone thinking that lowering taxes and cutting spending is going to control the growth of big government has got the cart before the horse.

No one must be listening, how many times I must say that nothing is going to stop the growth of government as long as it is in its social and family provider role. It must first be booted out of that all powerful social and family provider roles or it's always going to be an exercise in futility, period.

There is a reason why most of the world is dirt poor and will always be poor. The main reason is ignorant people just can't resist the crablike mentality, and in my view that is the main force that is driving and feeding this attack the rich self-destructive movement. The only way to bring power back to the people and the states is to completely get rid of the minimum wage, with all of my supernatural wisdom I can't think of any other way to get the welfare state out of its all powerful super family provider role.

SIRMANS LOG: 10 DECEMBER 2010, 1924 HOURS

WILL OBAMACARE SURVIVE?

UPDATE: 23 JANUARY 2011, 1243 HOURS.
What I see and understand so clearly on how an economy really work is simple, yet it shocks me why so few get it. Now almost everyone is focused on medical insurance, who got it, who can't get it, and on and on.

The Lib's rammed this Obamacare down our throats and believes that is the magic answer. I think all of that is missing the root problem with paying for medical care in America.

The root problem with medical care in America is "The lack of market forces due to the Federal government involvement." That involvement created the deadly side effect known as "Ultra-high-cost."

So, that makes "Mr. Ultra-high-cost" the real true villain in medical care. The government itself can't pay ultra-high-cost and 90 percent of the American people can't pay ultra-high-cost.

All any insurance company does is collect enough money from a lot of healthy well people and bet not too many of them will become sick at any one time.

Insurance companies won't have the money if more than just a few of their customers become sick at a time, which means they can't afford "Mr. ultra-high-cost."

So, the shallow minded liberals decided they would solve the whole problem by forcing every able body adult to pay for medical insurance or go to jail, which I think is a dictator tactic, and un-American.

They figured that would produce enough healthy well people paying into the system to satisfy "Mr. ultra-high-cost," and in theory that should work. But, that can never work when not enough people have jobs. Then it all boils down to the bottom line.

Before any business can make one red cent of profit or pay one employee's salary it first must pay a yearly business license fee, permit fees, federal income taxes, state income taxes, local option taxes, social security tax, unemployment tax, Medicare tax, state sales taxes, and taxes I can't even think of, plus satisfy all kinds of government red tape mandates.

Oh! I had forgotten to include having to make rent or mortgage payments too before the first penny of profit is made. I can't remember the statistics on the survival rate of all new startup businesses, but I think it is less than three percent still standing after five years.

On top of all of that everybody including the healthy young people is going to be hit with a new big whopping Obamacare health care tax.

Then and only then after paying all of that a business must try to find enough profit left to pay the employees, restock, take care of utilities, do maintenance and then live off what is left, it is no wonder why there are no jobs. Plus, some utility companies piles on by charging a business almost twice the rate that they do the public.

I believe when the Obamacare impact fully hits the jobless rate is going to sky rocket even higher than it is now, and then you add all of the welfare state dead beats that is a lot of people not paying into the system.

If Obamacare survives I just don't think there are going to be enough people paying into the system even if they do start giving the old folks pain pills and sending them on their way.

In fact at this stage I know beyond a shadow of doubt that eliminating the **"Minimum wage"** (www.FLSirmans.com/NoMinimumWageTest) and kicking the welfare state out of its social and family provider role is the only thing that's going to save the USA.

The family provider role must be restored back to the head of household where it belongs and where it always was until the "New deal" came along. That must be done or this great nation perishes.

Everyone keep griping about not making a living wage, but I will guarantee you that is a losing battle because the bigger the government the farther the cost of living out distances a living wage, there is no getting around that fact.

The only way to solve that is to get the government to stop giving out free money on an individual basis. If that is done the cost of living will have to come down to where poor people can pay their own medical bills and other cost, simply because the government will no longer be subsidizing and driving up prices.

Without the government subsidizing high prices by giving out free money on an individual basis very few merchant can charge more than the poor can pay and stay in business.

Sure, the government should help the poor and not let anyone starve, but do that by setting up temporary commissaries, kitchens, shelters, clinics, or whatever.

But, don't destroy the county's free market place, its culture, and everything else by giving out free money on an individual basis that is what ignited the killing inflation that is eating us alive today.

Right now no one wants to hear my no **"Minimum wage"** (www.FLSirmans.com/NoMinimumWageTest) solution, but they will, just wait, its coming, mass starving is right around the corner, you'll see.

Come on folks! Y'all got eyes and a brain! What goes here? Sometimes I wonder if the liberals really are this economically ignorant or just want go ahead and push this great nation on over the cliff. They are still speeding up government spending instead trying to cut back.

I know it's unthinkable, but what if they are trying to force martial law for a once and for all absolute government take over, government already owns 90 percent of the real estate market and big chunks of the manufacturing industry. Maybe I'm crazy to think out loud like this. Lord have mercy on my soul.

Using tunnel vision and looking at survival one dimensional through the economy prism only is the deadly mistake most egg heads and ninety five percent of the population are making.

All, even a real physical currency does is make trade and bartering a zillion times more convenient. Civilization has never survived only on faith and I don't believe it can today, and paper money is just that.

Civilization can and did survive on trade and bartering long before money was invented, but no society or nation is going to survive very long without all four legs of the survival stool holding strong, otherwise the nation will soon fall from within.

You can call it culture or whatever, but I see the first leg of the four legged survival stool as a strong nuclear and extended family system. The second leg I see as a strong moral and religious code in place.

The third leg I see as adequate bartering capacity backup in case the economy fails. That requires many small farmers and home gardeners, and with no citizen expecting the government to guarantee their survival.

And the fourth and last leg I see as the economy with a stable currency. Now, if anyone thinks we in the USA have a stable currency, good for you, I'm not so sure.

Being able to see all four legs of what I believe is the survival stool in perspective I think raises me above the tunnel vision and one dimensional thinking that so many so called smart people fall prey to.

Again, I write what I think, I don't try to tell anybody what to think, I might be a snake oil salesman myself for all you know. Do your own thinking and check more than one source.

If you don't see any validity in what I write just continue writing me off as a nut case and believe what the liberals tell you. Thank you for taking the time to read this article, and may God bless you. With love always, yours truly, bye.

SIRMANS LOG: 20 JANUARY 2011, 1736 HOURS.

Economic wise, all of the spending cuts and taxes remaining the same are going to do is take a smaller pie out of the oven. The only thing that is going to stop this runaway economy is booting the welfare state out of the all powerful social and family provider role, by eliminating the minimum wage as a first step. After the government first establish community wise only emergency kitchens, shelters, and clinics

A CURRENT EVENT ISSUE:
I saw on TV where two small minority talk radio hosts are going all out to try to destroy the biggest talk radio show host.

They say it is in the name of protecting the public from race baiting. I think what they fail to understand is what free speech is truly all about. Free speech is not just about what we agree with and want to hear, it is more about protecting that speech we disagree with and don't want to hear.

Hell, I feel anyone that genuine love and accept their own true self-identity will not feel threaten by every so called race baiting insensitive comment, because what is good for the goose is good for the gander.

I am already secure on who I am and stuff like that to me is like water off a ducks back. The key is to love and accept all people even if it is not returned, especially those of your own race who look like you.

No one is perfect and everyone has flaws, even if they don't show. Many, many people will totally disagree with everything I just said; still I have a right to say it under the five freedoms listed in the 1st amendment to the constitution of the United States of America.

SIRMANS LOG: ON THIS 69th PEARL HARBOR ANNIVERSARY DECEMBER 7, 1941, I WRITE THIS TODAY 1201 HOURS.

23 NOVEMBER 2010 1527 HOURS:

New update on air line search techniques.

I think the air lines, the workers, and all involved are trying their level best to make the best of a bad situation and keep the flying public safe.

Then on the other hand you have this negative constant drumbeat by much of talk radio and other arm chair quarter backs second guessing the best safety possible for the American flying public.

What this could end up doing is forcing the management into lesser security. Then guess what? Who do you think may end up taking much of the blame and heat if a plane ends up being blown out of the sky? Need I say more?

A CURRENT EVENT ISSUE: 22 NOVEMBER 2010, 2205 HOURS: New comment on air line search technique.

I think a few people are trying to keep a bandwagon going. Being patted down is not new, you go back over 40 to 50 year before modern metal detecting devices and it was not uncommon at all for some night clubs to do pat downs.

Its been over 50 years when I was a young man I along with everyone else was patted down before enter a night club and no one raised any hell about it.

No court is going to touch this with a ten foot pole, because then they would be responsible for what ever happens. The people raising so much hell don't have to answer for anything if a plane is blown up.

THE AIRLINES SEARCH TECHNIQUE!

Let me get this out of the way first, having the pilots go through the same search technique is nonsense in my view.

However, folks if not the strict search technique, what is your solution? Right now the same folks pissing and moaning the loudest will be the same ones complaining the loudest if their loved ones are on a plane that blows up.

Come on folks, no one has a gun to anyone's head telling them that they gotta fly. Take your voyage by ship or other means if it's that bothersome. What are you going to tell your urologist if you have a medical problem, it is the same with the intent not to be sexual in any way?

At the rate of technology advancement today a better remedy should come about very soon. But, until that happens, I say fly safe and live because it is not about any one individual.

I seen a lady on TV get all angry and rebellious, but, she could never come up with a real or better solution, which is the case with most of the get on the bandwagon complainers.

The vast majority of the people doing that type of work dislike the technique as much as you, but these people have family to feed. And their management has a responsibility to keep everyone alive. Talk is cheap.

F L SIRMANS, SR. PLEAS FOR DIVINE HELP!

The thing about me that make my great thinking so awesome is it is not limited in any way; it has no borders or boundaries. I have never been to economic school or taken any such classes! I don't know what is not supposed to work!

Almost all of my thinking is original; it is raw and creative from the core! Plus, my thinking takes in vastly more than the economic one leg of the whole survival stool. I'm more of a deep thinking philosopher that sees the whole survival stool and how the economy fits into the grand design.

There are infinite variables in an economy many are subjective which makes it impossible to be manage by man even with a super computer. What actually runs every economy no matter the type of government is nature's supreme law of "Natural selection."

Sure, almost any liberal bleeding heart do good economic system may work for 80-100 years, but, then the consequences of ignoring nature's supreme law of "Natural selection" catches up. And then someone is gonna pay in blood, sweat, or tears.

The nuclear and extended family system is the foundation of human survival. And is protected under nature's supreme law of "Natural selection."

So, when the welfare state for all practical purpose destroyed our nuclear and extended family system the consequences are going to make us pay dearly, hopefully we will survive as a nation.

I'm paraphrasing when I say someone complained that democracy was a terrible form of government but is still the best government known to man.

That is why I often wonder why is it so hard for nations to use an economic ideology that has never failed and have proven to always work time and time again. It will always produce an over abundance of everything.

That ideology is: "Allow free competition and let the free market place work." I think the real reason is governments just love power and the ability to control too much.

Another cold hard fact on that matter is: It is impossible to "Have free competition and a free market place" with government finger all in the pie. The more government gets involve the less of a free market place you will have.

When government sets a minimum wage which is like a vehicle with no reverse and enacts every kind or regulation and mandate one can imagine that means our USA economy doesn't even come close to being a free market place. That being the case, no one has to tell me that a total collapse is possible.

In the distance past a collapsing economy was something almost normal. It was just a rebirth or renewal. The strong nuclear and extended family system along with plenty bartering capacity would keep order until enough new growth kicked in.

We no longer have that safety valve anymore, western welfare states has just about destroyed that entire infrastructure. We no longer have a strong reliable nuclear and extended family structure anymore everybody is depending on our welfare state daddy.

Much of our moral and religious code has been reduced to what comes out of Hollywood. And we no longer have enough backup emergency bartering capacity in small farmers and home gardeners like what got us through the great depression.

This welfare state super beast has left this great nation with almost nothing in term of bare boned survival in time of crisis. We as a nation could face almost total chaos.

GOD, I ASK IN YOUR NAME, SAVE OUR GREAT NATION!
SIRMANS LOG: 9 NOVEMBER 2010, 1830 HOURS

MY QUICK BRIEF ANALYSIS OF

LIBERALISM!

I'm going to make a short brief analysis of liberalism and not make this a long drawn out detailed analysis. The first thing is there is nothing innate about being a liberal.

Liberalism is basically a lack of survival awareness. To put it more bluntly liberals tend to be shallow with a weak survival instinct. I'm not saying that to be mean and put down liberals in a negative way.

Life is about balance, no one thing in a person's life make one person better or lesser than another. I wouldn't want to live in a world without liberals because it would be too hard, cruel, and without the tender side of life.

Besides, many a liberal has been converted overnight to a conservative, especially if a mugger slammed them upside the head and robber them. I understand why liberals don't understand me and see me as some kind of kook or nut case.

The main reason is they can't see what I see. They don't have the depth and awareness that I have. I can see everything a liberal can see plus much, much more than a liberal will ever see simply because they have never fought a life time of mental battles like I have.

It is like buying a new car. All of a sudden you see cars of your make and model all over the place. Nothing has changed they were out there all of the while it's just that you were not aware of them. It is the same with knowing what it takes to survive.

If you have never had real test struggles on what it takes to survive you won't know what threats there are out there. That is why almost nothing of any real and lasting value can be accomplished without struggle and hardship.

I'm not special of have any kind of monopoly on wisdom. There are many people out there that have had it a lot worse than I have. And never forget that there is an exception to everything in nature. Hardship and struggle affects people in two ways.

It will make most people more humble and caring and overall a better human being. And a few it will make more and more bitter. I thank God it has made me a very humble and caring human being with super natural wisdom.

To fail to prepare a child how to be independent and stand on his own as a productive citizen eighteen years later is not real love and caring. That is irresponsible parenting!

BE THANKFUL INTO HIM, AND BLESS HIS NAME!
SIRMANS LOG: 8 NOVEMBER 2010, 0203 HOURS

SPENDING CUTS WON'T STOP THE DOOM OF WESTERN CIVILIZATION!
(keep scrolling down to read of the doom of western civilization)

7 NOVEMBER 2010, LAST UPDATE: 0839 HOURS
CURRENT EVENT:
I think both President Bush's 41 and 43 did a great job in protecting and safeguarding the Supreme Court. And I for one will forever sing their praise. But, I believe they both were good, proud and decent Rockefeller type republicans, also.

FOOLED BY THE GIFT OF GAB AND SLIGHT OF HAND!
The liberals are experts at the gift of gab and blame shifting but I will never be fooled because I watch more of what one does than a lot of false promises and empty rhetoric.

Liberals know they can never admit their true goals and intentions and get elected. The liberals are saying almost all of the right things, but, look at their action record for the last couple of years.

Their action record has been to grow big government like never before, not take any responsibility for their own actions, keep shifting all blame to someone else, government take over of most of the private auto industry, government take over of 90 percent of the private real estate market, screwing up the private insurance industry by almost doubling the price if you can still get it, and then to try to take over as much of the private sector as they can, which I believe is to make the USA a fully socialist country.

Their record is not hidden; it is right there for all to see what is really taking place in broad daylight. That is all the proof of liberal's intentions anyone need. God save this last bastion of true freedom in the world today.

I am under no illusion, I know the stuff I write is rejected by almost everyone, still, I must keep sounding the alarm even if no one takes heed.

I can assure you as long as government is a mass family provider nothing or no one is going to stop the growth of government. Sure, the tea party and conservatives will slow down the growth of government but they will find it impossible to stop all growth.

The reason is 95 percent of the American people don't see anything wrong with government in a provider role. There is no painless way to fix our economy and whoever actually makes painful drastic cuts are going to be voted out of office.

That is the pickle this nation is in. There has never been a nation that has changed course knowing it was headed toward disaster in the history of mankind. That is because those in power will never voluntarily release their death grip even if the nation goes down in flames.

The founding fathers put most of the real power in the hands of the people and the states, but, the people and the states gave up their real power.
The states gave up their real power by giving up the right to appoint two senate representatives every six years.

And the American people give up their real

power by allowing the federal government to seize and keep the family provider role for itself. Whoever carries out the family provider role is the boss and rules the country.

It hasn't finished consolidating it power yet, but the federal government already carries out a big enough percentage of the family provider role to stop all serious attempts at reducing its size. Very few government dependents are going to vote against the hand that feeds them.

This whole nation including the economy and everything else is now built around supporting one giant super welfare state beast. There is not enough money in the entire world to keep this beast fed.

But, if this beast is not fed our whole way of life will collapse into a giant dust heap, that is the pickle we are in. As I keep repeating with my great supernatural wisdom, the only controllable way to save this great nation with freedom still intact is to eliminate the minimum wage entirely, period.

We no longer have much of a choice; our whole economic system could collapse any day now. The first rule in economics is: you can't get blood out of a turnip.

That means no business can charge more than the poor people can afford to pay and stay in business because there is almost never enough rich and middle income people to keep a business profitable.

That is if government just stops subsidizing prices with welfare and food stamps and gets the hell out of the way. Then the price of everything and the ability to pay will seek a balance down where most of the poor can pay for their own food and medical cost out of pocket.

And those that can't pay should then have government run community shelters, kitchens, and clinics to turn to. The really sad thing is this nation's whole survival is at stake, and most people don't even have a clue.

CURRENT EVENT:
THE FIRING OF JUAN WILLIAMS!

I believe Juan Williams is a genuine liberal. I have seen him over the years on many programs. And I disagree with almost everything he says, yet I like Juan Williams.

In my view Juan Williams is no phony yes man that always goes along to get along. I think he is loved and respected by so many because it shines through that he is a truly honest and decent man.

Again, I almost totally disagree with him on everything, but, it is in my nature to respect decency and honesty no matter who has it. I think Juan Williams has that and no one can take that asset away.

I seldom comment on current events, but on this matter I felt a need to weigh in.

ABOUT SPENDING CUTS!

Spending cuts won't save welfare state economies because that is not striking at the heart of the matter. The root of the problem is government cannot take on the nuclear family provider role on a large scale without destroying the culture and everything in it.

All spending cuts are going to do is pit one group against another and speed up the process to doom. Right now all four legs of the survival stool are beginning to collapse. The whole system is out of balance due to violations of nature's supreme law of "natural selection."

It is those consequences that are now catching up with us. There are no free rides in nature someone always pays one way or another. The violations started with the "New deal" when government seized the nuclear and family provider role for itself but failed to maintain family discipline.

The liberals done this to keep power by handing out goodies with tax payers money and is still trying to keep it up to this day. That was the poison pill that is about to kill our economy around 80 years later. There is no saving western civilization until government is kicked out of the nuclear and extended family provider role, period.

Money or the lack of money today is not everything but seem to be the only thing that matters. But, the truth is civilization survived with trade and bartering long before money was invented.

The four legs of the survival stool are: (1.) The nuclear and extended family system, (2.) a strong religious and moral code, (3.) adequate emergency bartering capacity with many small farmers and home gardeners, and (4.) the economy and money with a physical backed currency.

Now, everyone is zeroing in on cutting spending, especially social spending. I urge caution, when the government has irresponsible created masses upon masses of dependents with no knowledge of how to survive solely on their own it cannot just walk away.

These people need to be conditioned to be responsible and think for themselves. Government must provide on a wide scale community wise emergency shelters, kitchens, and clinic. There is no doubt in my mind if the government gets out of the way the free enterprise system with entrepreneurs will save the USA with its freedom intact.

But, one way or another government must give up its nuclear and extended family provider role or all is lost. No matter what the egg heads tell you, I guarantee you this ship is going down unless the minimum wage is gotten rid of entirely, I can't see any other way.

After first establishing community wise emergency shelters, kitchens, and clinics, then by eliminating the minimum wage it will allow a slow manageable means of avoiding a total collapse of the whole system. A total collapse could mean 100 million or more starving to death.

With all of my great wisdom on the line that is my analysis of the situation we as a nation are in. To not pass this on in my view would be a dialect of duty on my part. No one has to believe me or even take me serious.

If you think I'm a kook or my analysis is totally crap I assure you not everyone thinks as you do. What is your solution? If you have a better one, please share it, I have a comment section on my website.

The sun shall not smite thee by day nor the moon by night.
SIRMANS LOG: 21 OCTOBER 2010, 1055 HOURS

HOW TO DEFUSE OUR WELFARE STATE DESTRUCTION TIME BOMB!
(Keep scrolling down to read time bomb article)

15 OCTOBER 2010: LAST UPDATE, 0819 HOURS

Having the USA government fulfilling the role of the "Great white father" super colossal social and family provider is like having the fox guarding the hen house.

There is no way our all power welfare state is going to continue tolerating individual freedom in the USA because it already has the power to tax at will and take what it wants to continue ruling over us like we are peons.

The Supreme Court and no law are going to stop it unless the minimum wage is completely eliminated, period. Then the people can take back the family provider role for themselves and the government will be dependent on the will of the people like the founding fathers designed it.

CURRENT EVENT:
A SUPER COLOSSAL MISTAKE IN MY VIEW!

I think one of the dumbest and naive political moves I've seen lately is the denying being a witch political Ad. All that did was focus on the negative and give legs to something no one would have given a damn about except the shallow liberal news media.

Instead of her relentlessly pounding on no jobs and too high taxes which is a sure winner she allowed herself to be sucked into the mire of a juicy personal issue by trying to disprove a negative, which is almost impossible. Still, it's better late than never to right the ship.

My unsolicited advice is get out front, let the voters decide, don't be shy, ask them which political party will most likely control wasteful spending and help the private sector provide real lasting jobs, not big government temporary make work jobs.

The obvious political party that will do all of that is a no brainier, let the voter decides. Whoever wins, hopeful the people will have heard both sides and not one side drowned out by a lot of emotional nonsense?

STAY ON MESSAGE, LOWER UNEMPLOYMENT AND LOWER TAXES AND DON'T GET SIDE TRACKED!
Most candidates get side tracked because of the mass news media.

The media will bite on just about anything and run like hell with it if there is even a hint of smut or dirt involved. But, obsessing on juicy and personal stuff leaves voters without a sensible option and in almost all cases works against a conservative.

The liberals will go to the extreme in tossing the media some bait to help lure a conservative away from lower taxes and more jobs. I believe the Brown case is an example of trying to keep the focus away from high unemployment and too high taxes.

A word to the wise, don't let the personal stuff throw you off message. The majority Productive citizen cares far more about more jobs and less taxes than who did who. HELLO?

Keep the drum beat going louder and louder for more jobs and less taxes no matter how loud the personal distractions is blasted about you, then you can't lose with the stuff you use.

HOW TO DEFUSE OUR WELFARE STATE DESTRUCTION TIME BOMB!

Okay, let's get real and face the rock hard cold steel facts. Starting with the "New deal" the liberals from both major political parties has created our big government monster size social and family provider beast.

It has created countless government dependents with many depended on government for their only survival. What surprises and scares the hell out of me is around 95 percent of the American people don't see anything wrong with government being a super family provider and think that is normal.

Nothing could be farther from normal; it's insane for government to be a family provider in a free country. No free country will remain free with government in the all powerful role of super family provider.

Going back over 5000 years until the "New deal" came along the nuclear and extended family system always maintained with discipline the family provider role, then liberals in the name of government seized it for themselves solely to dish out goodies to keep power.

But, government refused to set standards, and then family discipline went out the window especially in the African American community. And even to this day no one is instilling self-restraint in most black males and they are filling up the prisons at an ever increasing rate.

I can't make you believe me but I'm still going to tell you the gospel truth anyway, there is no way in hell the USA is ever going to be saved from doom without rebuilding the nuclear family system as part of any solution. Now, chew on that!

Whoever is the family provider is the boss and has almost unlimited power over its dependents and in this case the voters. Whoever is your provider is your boss like it or not no matter how you spin it.

The only power we the people have left in America is our vote and that is practically useless in a real showdown because very few government dependents are going to bite the hand that feeds them.

Right now, you hear the Tea party talk and the talk about voting one team out and putting in a new slower team, drip, drip, dripping still ever so slowly toward full socialism. What we need is a halt and then a retreat no matter how slowly away from socialism.

But, until I actually see a retreat I believe it is still all talk because practically all of the real power is still in the hands of our all powerful sugar daddy welfare state provider. Really, do you people actually believe a new team in place is going to put a dent in social spending?

It has never been done in the past and I bet my bottom dollar it ain't gonna happen this time if we get a new team running the show. Sure, there will be a lot of talk and promises but nothing will have any real teeth in my view.

Around the world you see labor unions and others rioting in the street when even the smallest cut or changes are planned. Well, the same thing is going to happen in America when real change is seriously proposed. And for now I just don't think the voters are quite ready to do what must be done for this nation to survive.

There simply is no painless way out of the burdens and responsibilities the liberals have taken on for this nation to have to bear. I know the future may look hopeless but all is not lost. But, it's going to require some great wisdom I, Freddie L. Sirmans, Sr. can provide.

Whatever is done to save this great nation from total destruction must utilize the "Natural selection" process. Any piece meal cuts here and there are going to pit one group against the other to no end.

Forget about who may lose this or that the existence and survival of the nation itself is at stake. There is no avoiding deflation, plus deflation itself is not a bad thing, avoiding deflation is what got us in this dire mess in the first place.

The thing about deflation is it is harmless

and healthy if brought about in a "Natural selection" process. On the other hand if it is managed solely by man it could mean everyone going for each others throat and total chaos.

Okay, first things first, before action is taken the goal should be to return the family provider role back to where it belongs with the nuclear and extended family system. If that is not the goal there is nothing I can do to help save this great nation.

If the goal is to save this great nation by returning the provider role back where it belongs, here is my propose plan of action: Government should prepare by first setting up all around the country community wise only emergency shelters, kitchens, and clinics.

Once that is done, completely eliminate the minimum wage entirely, period. That will through the "Natural selection" process slowly start deflating the entire economy in a manageable way, however, there will be survival growing pains, but they will be bearable, the economy and country will survive with freedom still intact.

There will be many, many, more jobs and the whole system will start correcting itself. The whole process depends on the government returning the provider role back to a quickly rebuilding nuclear and extended family system and letting the private sector rebuild the free market place.

Government should focus on internal and external defense, community wise shelters, kitchens, and clinics, and collecting a lot less in taxes needed. Deflation will bring about a balance where all prices will start coming down to where the average working man and woman can live and pay their own medical cost out of pocket. It is not the amount of money that counts it's the buying power of money that truly matters.

This is my solution to help save this great country from collapsing into total chaos. If anyone else has a better solution step forward, then dismiss my plan of action. A word of advice, keep listening to the eggs heads that keep spouting the big government line and we all are going to be up S... creek without a paddle.

He that keepeth thee will not slumber.
SIRMANS LOG: 29 SEPTEMBER 2010, 2049 HOURS.

<u>A CHICKEN WITH ITS HEAD CUT</u>

OFF ANALOGY!
(Scroll farther down for chicken with head cut off analogy)

The scariest thing in the world for a liberal is to get caught in a position where there is no one else to blame and he has take responsibility. To try to get a liberal to avoid shifting blame is like shoving a cross in the face of a vampire.

I really don't like to dwell too much on me when I write but there is a time for everything and I will be brief concerning me.

I know I don't have any real power to change anything or convince anyone else to make changes, however, no matter how small, I do believe I am offering enlightenment which can be a life line for this nations survival.

There is no doubt in my mind that I'm right on the vast majority of my analyses. I feel sooner or later more people will realize the validity of my great wisdom to aid in the survival of this great nation.

If I'm wrong I will continue to be almost completely ignored as a kook. But, if I'm truly right as I say I am all of the king's horses and all of the kings men are not going to be able to keep my talent and abilities from seeking their own level of greatness.

If God willing and the creek don't rise I will stay the course because persistent and determination alone are omnipotent. "My help cometh from God, he will not suffer thy foot to be moved."

No American business man wants to leave his own country and take away American jobs. But, first a business must survive both its competition and the ability to make a profit or it cease to exist.

What is really driving Americans jobs out of the country is the appetite demand of our welfare state to fund its super social and family provider role. The truth is the social and family provider role belongs to first the Nuclear and extended family system, the church, and community organizations, period.

As a last resort government should help out but only on a temporary basis. That has been the foundation for civilizations survival for over 5000 years until the "New deal" came along. I'm telling you economics is just one leg of the survival stool and it's not the most important one either.

If a nation doesn't have a dependable nuclear and extended family system in place along with a good moral and religious code no amount of money is going to save it from doom.

Yet, I hear the liberals blaming everybody and his brother for America's financial problems when they are the ones to blame for creating this super welfare state beast that want to provide cradle to grave care for everyone with tax payers money.

Hell, I would be for big government taking care of me and everybody, too, but I have sense enough to know it's impossible and it will destroy the country. Get a grip America before the liberals leave us all to perish.

Have you ever seen a chicken run around with its head cut off, I have and it's not a pretty sight?

I was born in 1942 and we lived on a farm. Many times I have seen my mother kill a chicken for dinner. There was sort of a chopping block in a back yard that you couldn't find a blade of grass anywhere.

My mother would fire up a huge pot of

boiling water then go out to the hen yard and grab a pullet. She would take the pullet by both legs and hold its neck over that block, and then she would take a large machete like butcher knife and whack the head off with one swing.

She would then quickly sling the chicken out into the yard; the chicken would land on its feet and run headless like crazy in all directions for several seconds. The hot boiling water would permit the feathers to be easily pulled off.

Today most people don't realize it but anytime we eat meat someone had to perform a violent act necessary for our survival. That is what all of this activity involving the economy reminds me of. Almost everyone is running every which a way trying to come up with a solution.

I can guarantee you what the problem is in four words and it is what's destroying both the USA culture and economy, but reason and sanity has flown the coop; reality has yet to set in. And until these four words I'm talking about are dealt with nothing is going to work.

Way back before the nuclear weapon age of mutual destruction the authoritarian non-free market place governments survived by exploiting smaller and weaker states. Non-free market place states have never been able to feed its entire population except through slavery of some other type of exploitation.

Today no country can survive without a free market place unless it has natural resources to sell or receive outside help. "Government as a provider" is the four words I'm talking about and is the arch-villain that have all but destroyed our culture and economy.

Once government seized the provider role for itself and got drunk on the godlike power as a super provider, it don't ever plan on going back to just protecting and defending the country and doing only the things the people can't do for themselves.

As long as government is still in its super provider role we the people might as well kiss this great land of the free goodbye because nothing less than kicking government out of that role is going to save the USA from doom.

When government is in the role of super provider it has practically all of the real power and it is going to use that power to consolidate and protect that power, the country, manufacturing, jobs and everything else can go straight to hell as long as its provider role is protected.

You mark my words nothing less than kicking the government out of its super provider role is going to amount to a hill of beans.

Sure, government has a responsibility to help keep people alive by providing community wise things like community shelters, community kitchens, and community clinics, but anything more destroys the "Natural selection" need for the nuclear and extended family system. And that is the worst thing you can do to any society, because when the nuclear and extended family system goes culture decline soon follows, then the economy stalls and finally total doom.

When the nuclear and extended family can't help an individual then to the rescue should be the church and community organizations, and if all of that fails only then should the government help with community wise facilities.

There must be a survival need for the nuclear and extended family system or it will cease to exist. A welfare state destroys that need. Kicking the government out of it provider role is all it will take for the USA to survive and regain its greatness because nothing else is going to save us from total doom.

I know my God given great wisdom will be totally ignored but still I've did my duty. In life there are no free rides, sooner or later the day to pay the piper can't be put off any longer and must be paid in blood, sweat, or tears.

The energy and force that is driving this whole world wide decline of western civilization is the mostly big government liberals that are dead set on making more and more people government dependent.

Everything spins off of that driving force, you name it, high taxes, jobs going over seas, illegal immigrants, and every other ill of today is a direct result of liberals determines to finance their social and family provider role.

It is an impossible task because as more and more dependents are made you have fewer and fewer people paying into the system. Still, the liberals keep fooling enough voters with big promises and smooth talk to stay in power, what a sad situation.

I'm fixing to say something about me that is

probably my wild imagination gone astray, but still it just may be an ounce of truth in it. Here goes, it is mind boggling how a shy neurotic insecure poor South Georgia USA country boy with only a high school formal education can raise up out of the ashes like a phoenix and influence world wide economic thinking.

That is truly a miracle that only destiny can bring about, if you doubt me just read some of my books found on any Internet search engine, Alias Freddie L Sirmans, Sr.

My miracle could never have happen before the Internet age. I agree my books may not always be top notch professionally written because everything is done solely by me. The formatting and grammar may not always meet the highest standard. But, none of that stops my supernatural great wisdom from shinning through.

When it comes to the bare bone survival of this nation many of my answers and solutions are unsurpassed. I believe what is at stake here is the survival of western civilization and capitalization itself.

I also believe my deep, deep wisdom bores through all of the smoke, fog and others distractions and strikes at the heart of the arch-villain (Government as a provider) that is about to take down the USA and western civilization.

Unless this villain is shot with a silver bullet or an iron stake driven through the heart the American people will never be able to regain enough power to stop this welfare state beast from selling this country's sovereignty to the U.N. or some new world body.

Sure, I'm going to be called a kook, nut case, and a host of other mentally disturbed names but still none of that will proves me wrong. Only History can prove me wrong and the wait won't be very much longer because I believe this whole global economy is on the brink of collapsing.

When you read my writing it is raw, crude, extreme, and undiluted by any editor or anyone just like when you drink your liquor straight with no chaser, only the rough and tough can take it.

I will lift up mine eyes unto the hills from whence cometh my help.
SIRMANS LOG: 6 SEPTEMBER 2010, 1721 HOURS.

<u>THERE IS NO SUCH THING AS AN</u>

ANCHOR BABY!
WHY LIBERALS ARE BEWILDERED AND IN A PANIC ABOUT THE ECONOMY! UPDATED: SIRMANS LOG: 18 AUGUST 2010, 2049 HOURS.

The liberals don't understand it and is in a funk as to why the economy is not responding to their mass spending. What is the problem in their minds, they are using the same technique that have successful fooled the people for over one half century to keep their power.

They know the general public and average American doesn't have a clue as to the basic of how an economy really works. Throwing gasoline on a fire will instantly cause a big fire but that is not the same as adding logs that will keep a lasting fire.

Well, it is the same with the economy; the first thing liberals will do is create mass social spending and construction projects which are like pouring gasoline on a fire. And sure enough in the past it would boom the economy for a few years.

Hurrah, hurrah, from the man/woman on the street any boom no matter the cost is proof enough for them to keep voting the big spenders back in office. The down side to using this irresponsible technique to gain and keep power is it keeps growing government bigger and bigger.

Now, we have on our hand a super big government welfare state beast. Remember, all government income and I mean all originates from some form of business profit from the private sector.

I believe the tax bite, permit fees, license fees, and every other type of government mandate into a businesses profit have become so big that fewer and fewer can survive, let alone hire new people. A law of nature is you can squeeze a tax payer lemon only so many times before there is no more juice.

Yet, the liberals are still trying to boom the economy with that same old technique of mass new social spending and construction. The difference now is instead of booming the economy it is putting more and more people out of work, wake up America. But, that is not the end of the story.

What that irresponsible technique has done over the years is for all practically purpose destroyed our culture. We have no strong and dependable nuclear and extended family system. Our moral and religious code is almost in total ruins, with homosexual and every other type porn everywhere and even in reach of many of our kids.

We don't even have any underground bartering capacity to speak off, that have always existed in a nation of free people, the welfare state beast even took that away by making us so dependent minded, we have unshakable faith in uncle sugar for cradle to grave care.

It is a simple fact we don't have enough small farmers and home gardeners growing their own food, and its going to cause mass starvation when this global economy crash.

God, I ask in your name please continue to bless this last bastion of true freedom in the world today.

THERE IS NO SUCH THING AS AN ANCHOR BABY!

I've heard the term "Anchor babies" but what concerns me is a few conservatives are being take in by that and the banning of the "Born in America automatic citizenship."

I think it is bad idea and I'm totally against banning something that has worked just fine for over 200 years. Right now it is about illegal immigrants and proving their right to be here, but by banning the "born in America automatic citizenship" it could come down to every American having to prove he has a right to be here.

Just because a baby is born in the USA doesn't give an illegal immigrant parent the right to stay here. A baby can't provide and take care of itself so the baby must remain with the parent if deported.

I'm just glad I don't have to make the decision to deport a new American citizen along with an illegal immigrant parent. I can only speak for me just one individual but I believe banning the "Born in America automatic citizenship" could open up a whole new can of worms.

Families that have been here ever since slavery may have to prove they have a right to be here. However, if the immigrant laws now in the book are not being enforced it really doesn't matter if a baby is a USA citizen or not he/she is still living in America. **SIRMANS LOG: 16 AUGUST 2010, 2245 HOURS.**

ARE WE SUICIDAL AS A NATION? UPDATED: SIRMANS LOG: 12 AUGUST

2010, 1129 HOURS.
LIBERALS WILL NEVER PHYSICAL CUT FOOD STAMPS!

If this is an attempt to move to the middle it sure is a dumb way to go about it. I don't get it, because to the man/woman on the street perception is reality.

If you are telling me the liberals in Washington D.C. are actually going to cut food stamps, I'm telling you it ain't gonna happen. Something like this will make the poor mad and end with even more contempt from the hard working tax payers.

I for one think federal, state, and local government should privatize out of their sugar daddy social and family provider roles entirely. But, not before government set up mass community wise only emergency kitchens, shelters, and clinics first.

That will allow time for a strong nuclear and extended family system to rebound and save this great nation from total doom. Then if taxes were cut to the bone and red tape restricted it would free entrepreneurs to save our economy and the country from total doom.

UPDATED: SIRMANS LOG: 8 AUGUST 2010, 1210 HOURS.

In a true free market place economy it is impossible for prices or anything else to get out of reach for the poor unless the government gets involved and screws everything up.

Natures supreme law of "Natural selection" will make sure the poor will be able to pay out of pocket for their own doctor bills, especially with nuclear and extended family help. Otherwise, when the government tries to provide care and help for everyone it starts an inflationary cycle by forcing businesses to charge higher and higher prices to pay higher and higher taxes to the government.

That whole process is called the welfare state and in the end hurts the poor and everyone by destroying the nuclear family, small farmers, and eventually the country.

When the federal government tries to provide and care for everybody then nature's supreme law of "Natural selection" is going to destroy the federal government itself unless it jettisons its far too heavy financial load.

I predict unless the federal government jettisons most of the financial burdens it has now we will have a crash within two years because our economic engine is already in full stall.

ARE WE SUICIDAL AS A NATION?

Over and over time and time again, still, I feel the need to say it again, it is impossible for man to manage successful a free market economy, Nature's supreme law of "Natural selection" is what controls every economy in the final analysis. All man can do to guarantee a successful economy is allow free competition and let the free market place work its magic; it has never failed in the history of mankind.

Yet, the egg head modern economist's keeps trying to do the impossible. It boggles my mind why a neurotic uneducated South Georgia USA country boy can see the big picture so clearly and dissect an economy down to where even a fool can understand it.

The people running the country aren't stupid. It pains me to see us eating the last of our seed corn and drinking the last of our priming water, we will have no way to recover and no way to survive, still I'm seen as a fool and nut case.

All I hear is money, money, and the need to spend more money. What good is more money for the nation when our welfare state beast has already almost completely destroyed our nuclear family system and our once strong religious and moral code?

We are living on borrowed time. There is an old saying that love is the only things that people will willingly give up their life for. Another old saying is the worst thing you can do to a free country is create conditions where rich people can't hold on to their money. Their loyalty is the glue that holds every free society together.

I don't care how much you pay someone to provide care; it will never equal nuclear family care. I don't care how many bailouts are given it will never replace earned business profit. The more financial burdens the government takes on the more business profit it has to take to pay new bills.

The more profit a business has to share with the government the less it will have left to produce paid employees that will be paying taxes to the government. When the government business tax bite become to great all economic growth ceases, still, our welfare state beast keep adding more burdens and spending like there is no tomorrow.

Even an idiot should know that a collapse is going to happen, or there may be forces out there that would welcome a collapse along with a chance to seize absolute power. Otherwise, the nation must be mad, insane, in denial, or just plain suicidal.
SIRMANS LOG: 6 AUGUST 2010, 2203 HOURS.

WHY IS THE FEDERAL GOVERNMENT SO OUT OF PHASE WITH THE AMERICAN PEOPLE ON IMMIGRATION?

With the Arizona court case going on the question often asked is: Why is the federal government so against the thinking of most of the American people? I'll tell you why in simple terms.

The quick answer is instinct; this big government welfare state by instinct is against conservatism and anything it feels is a threat to its super provider role.

Big government as a super sugar daddy provider holds the reins and by instinct knows the welfare state cannot survive without Mexican laborers no matter their legal status.

Liberals live in the now and see the tomorrow as time to find a way to place all blame on some one else. Their one and only concern is to protect and keep their God like super provider role and to hell with individual freedom, the American people, or anything else that threatens their power.

The big government liberals knows we will never get enough Americans to do the hard hot farm work with our current welfare state, these people are not stupid, but, the welfare state is their God and source of power and they will sell their soul and country to protect it.

I believe starting with the "New deal" the liberals has been more successful than even they realize. They has successful destroyed almost everything necessary for America to remain a civilized nation.

When the need for your nuclear family system, your religious and moral code, and your emergency bartering capacity are all taken away by this liberal sugar daddy welfare state that alone in my view is damn near Armageddon.

No one, not even one with a pee wee survival instinct would place the fate of 300 millions people in something as unstable as any government, God must be staying his hand, the liberals know not what they have done to this great nation. In your name God I ask, please continue to bless this great nation.

There are no free rides in life someone somehow always pays in blood, sweat, or tears sooner or later. All of those babies killed in the womb must be accounted for in the eyes of nature.
SIRMANS LOG: 28 JULY 2010, 1910 HOURS.

<u>WHY I BELIEVE MOST AFRICAN AMERICANS ARE LOCKED INTO DEPENDENCY MODE.</u>

Most African Americans view my type of thinking as threatening and view me as a sell-out and Uncle Tom. They are wrong. In the eyes of nature survival takes top priority and anything else can be dealt with later.

I still believe in the true American dream in the old fashion way and that don't include a welfare state with guaranteed results to anyone. However, I do believe in guaranteed freedom and opportunity for all.

For survival I believe one should depend on

self, the extended family, the church, the community, and the government only as a last resort, and then only on a temporary basis. Coming out of slavery my type of thinking would have been very dangerous and would have made it a lot harder for blacks to survive, especially in the Deep South.

So, from a survival point of view it was a good thing for blacks to acquire a dependency mentality. But, that was then, it is now time for African Americans to stop sucking on that same titty, man up and take responsibility for our own actions and save our own neighborhoods. No one else is going to do it.

The liberals got us black's right where they want us as a loyal dependable voting block in their favor. It is not in their best self-interest to help the black community become too independent and self-sufficient.

I will sum it up by saying: Before an individual or a people can think and act responsible in ones own community self-interest they first must break out and escape a dependency mode of thinking.

In my view very few African Americans has been able to do that mainly because of our sugar daddy welfare state. The welfare state destroyed our nuclear and extended family system and keeps African Americans and the poor irresponsible and moral corrupt as a whole.

The poor have never killed babies in the womb until this welfare state came along. Very few people are willing to hire young blacks to do domestic work in their home because of the trust factor. Doing domestic work played a big role in African Americans surviving coming out of slavery.

As I have said many times the economy is only one leg of the four legged survival stool, the other three legs are the nuclear and extended family, a strong religious and moral code, and adequate backup bartering capacity. The egg heads running the nations economy knows I'm right but will never admit it.

SIRMANS LOG UPDATED: 27 JULY 2010, 1106 HOURS.

THE GREAT QUESTION?

QUESTION: Why do intelligent reasonable educated people continue to be suckered by smooth talking pie in the sky liberals? The same question is asked when people are flim flamed, how anyone could fall for something so obviously snake oil tonic.

The same common thread is found in all cases, the victim is expecting something for nothing. An independent do-for-yourself individual will become alert and suspicious the minute someone promises to make life a bed of roses.

To all of those expecting big changes in the next election, it may happen but remember the welfare state has made most Americans big government dependents to some degree.

Sure, the Tea party members and a few others have seen the light, but still the big concern of far too many Americans is "What has government done for me lately." The real problem is people just don't understand the basics of what make an economy work including the news media and most economists.

The people can see jobs leaving the country and fewer and fewer jobs being produced. But, they can't make the leap and understand why jobs are leaving and why jobs are not being produced. The sole reason for a business to exist is to make a profit to survive.

The first thing a business must survive is its

competition and that can't be done if the competition is using cheaper labor.

The people see the good the government does like helping the poor, the elderly, the handicap, the disadvantage, and so many good deeds, but they can't see that all personal and government income is derived from business profit. And when you kill business profit by taking too much you kill the country.
SIRMANS LOG: 21 JULY 2010, 0132 HOURS.

HOW TO CREATE JOBS!
UPDATED: 6 JULY 2010, 1116 HOURS.
The stupid thing about becoming too government dependent in a free country is sooner or later every government is going to run out of money, or the ability to borrow.

The USA is almost there, good men has stood by and let the liberals create this welfare state beast that has destroyed our nuclear family system, our breadbasket small farmers, and lastly any emergency capacity to barter.

Those things are the basic of every civilized society and for their loss the USA is going to pay dearly in pain, suffering, and starving.

The great wisdom found in Freddie L. Sirmans, Sr's books and writings lay out the wisest course to take.

Privatizing government out of its super social and family provider role is the first thing that must be done. Next, the minimum wage must be completely eliminated and all taxes cut to the bone, that will then set entrepreneurs free to feed and save America.

I have too much wisdom and common sense to be taken serious in this insane economic atmosphere, my great wisdom and sound judgment will be written off as the ranting and raving of a lunatic.

I say to hell with the party line and following any be happy economic propaganda over a cliff, because if we stay on the course we are on America will not survive.

Anyone with an ounce of economic wisdom will know that I'm right. Actually, the jig is up. If we don't move fast and get out front on this, nature's law of "Natural selection" will to do it its way, which is cold, brutal, and unforgiving.

HOW TO CREATE JOBS!
With my great wisdom I will give you a very

simple answer that has withstood the test of time and is guaranteed to work. Jobs are created by those with the funds and resources who want to and expect to make a profit.

If you take away any one of those ingredients jobs won't be created. The biggest culprit that is hindering job creation is big government by taxing away job producing business profit.

Making a profit is the only thing that can generate wealth. Sure, power can take from others or make others work for free and acquire wealth but only profit can generate wealth.

The problem with the USA economy and the global economy is it is like a vehicle with no reverse and that is stupid; no one would buy a car with no reverse.

That has created a false conception in most Americans that more and more money is the answer, wrong. It is not the amount of money but the buying power of money that is most important.

If it takes $50.00 to buy what we use to buy for $5.00 we have lost ground instead of gained ground in terms of buying power which is like a dog chasing its own tail, read Freddie L. Sirmans, Sr's books and writing on how to save America.

Big Government as a social and family provider has locked the USA and Europe into a global economic system that requires higher and higher taxes to support bigger and bigger government in a never ending inflationary spiral.

Around and around it goes with each tax increase cutting deeper and deeper into a business's profit until nothing is left. Plus, as government gets bigger and bigger the red tape hurdle on getting into business becomes almost insurmountable.

While all of this is going on you have masses of people bitching and moaning wondering why there are no jobs. Yet, these same people keep voting the big spending liberals in office to take care of everybody. Guess what, all personal and government income comes from some form of business profit.

It is very simple, the harder it is for a business to make a profit, the harder it is for people to find jobs. Also, the more business profit the government takes the fewer businesses can survive to provide tax paying jobs.

The end result is it is impossible for government to survive very long as a social and family provider, period. There is simply no way a welfare state can survive over 80-100 years, the drag and load becomes impossible to carry.

These same people think I'm stupid and uncaring when I say completely get rid of the minimum wage and kick the government out of its social and family provider role.

They forget the first priority is food, shelter, and staying warm. And no civilization has ever been able to do that without a strong nuclear and extended family system, along with adequate bartering capacity in small farmers and home gardeners, which our sugar daddy welfare state has almost destroyed.

A healthy free market place economy should be able to seek its own level like a liquid. By government invading the free market place and propping up prices that is what put prices out of reach for almost everyone, otherwise the poor with their numbers along would halt inflation.

This economy is about to crash but don't expect anything to change. Practically our whole culture and way of thinking now is to look to the government instead of to self, the nuclear and extended family, and lastly the government.

Until the "New deal" came about around eighty years ago, going back over 5,000 years people depended on themselves, the nuclear and extended family, the church, the community, and almost never on government to survive.

You can get into ideology, different types of government, or whatever, but unless there is a profit incentive no economic system is going to work, there are no exceptions in the history of man kind. I predict mass starving in the USA and around the world soon. However, I pray that I'm wrong. **SIRMANS LOG: 1 JULY 2010, 0120 HOURS.**

A BASIC HUMAN NATURE AND ECONOMIC LECTURE!

The reason why liberals will always destroy wealth and freedom in a country is because their shallow do good intention makes them want to take all risk and failure out of life.

The shallow naive flaw in that type of

thinking is human's beings is not cogs in a machine we are motivated by a complex reward or punishment response behavior. It is a law of nature that success and failure goes hand in hand and you can't have one without the other.

Just as it is as important to be able to forget things as it is to remember things but hardly anyone thinks about it that way, all of the focus is on remembering. So, when big government and the liberals prevent small purges and failures it puts the whole system at risk.

That shuts off any way to control inefficiency, crud, moral decay, and all negative anti-survival forces. Then it is only a matter of time before the negative forces of inefficiency and moral decay grow too powerful for human survival.

Also, it is impossible to create great wealth in a nation without someone willing to take a great risk and no one is going to be willing to take a great risk without individually expecting a great reward, liberals ignore this fact.

That is the reason communism and socialism will never produce wealth and riches because everyone will try to exert the least amount of energy to receive an equal reward, and that is simply human nature.

What I've said is basic kindergarten human nature knowledge; still most liberals can't comprehend these facts. A hundred years ago just day to day survival made almost everyone aware of these fact, but not since the "New deal."

It is so sad just how shallow most Americans have become since the "New deal" and our all powerful sugar daddy welfare state has become the cradle to grave great white father super provider.

Soon when this great white father super provider is broke and has a red tape death grip on all self initiative, what are we to do? God help us break this death grip and survive.

God I ask in your name give us the wisdom and strength to survive in spite of what the well intention do good liberals has unknowingly done to this great country. **SIRMANS LOG: 25 JUNE 2010, 2149 HOURS.**

<u>MASS FUEL SAVING VEHICLES AIN'T GONNA HAPPEN IN THE USA!</u>

UPDATED: 19 JUNE 2010, 1854 HOURS. MASS FUEL SAVING VEHICLES AIN'T GONNA HAPPEN IN THE USA!

The technology to produce a vehicle that would cut fuel consumption almost in half has been around ever since the late 1950's. From an economically point of view there are thousands of things made from oil from the pavement we drive on to the clothes on our backs, but fuel consumption is the lions share.

The reason no genuine serious effort to produce a mass fuel saving vehicle is not going to happen is because big business and the government wants more profit and revenue not less. Sure, there is some fiddling around and pretending to make a mass produced fuel saving vehicle but that is just throwing out a bone to fool the public.

If you think I'm wrong about a fuel saving vehicle take a look at the diesel locomotive. Two or three diesel locomotives can pull hundreds of box car all day long without gulping fuel. The reason is they have no drive train. The diesel engine powers a generator that supplies electrical power to electric motors for the wheels. And it's been that way ever since the late 1950's.

Sure, automobiles need quick acceleration

for passing but with technology a way could be found to overcome that. All I'm saying is that in the real world what saves or works best don't always win out.

To sum it up, once the "New deal" gave the government an excuse to seize the nuclear family provider role for itself the destruction of the USA economy die was cast, estimated collapse time 4-6 generations into the future. As a super social and family provider the government is going to fight tooth and nails any and every decrease in revenue.

That is why government as a family provider will never allow a free people to remain free for very long. I have been out here screaming and hollering about the dangers of the welfare state to deaf ears now for many years.

But, I believe time is winding down and more and more of my great wisdom is going to be realized and appreciated. I thank you God for my life, health, and strength. I carry on and refuse to stand down America.

I'm at a loss as how to think and act any other way. I give God the Praise, thank you God, thank you, thank you...

IMMIGRATION HYPOCRITES GALORE! Scroll down to read article

WRITERS OPINION ON STATES POWER!

I believe the main reason why the 10th amendment is totally ignored today is because of the passing of the 17th amendment. It wasn't obvious at the time but it has destroyed the balance of power between the federal government and the states.

In a real showdown the states no longer has any real power in congress because the senate is now mostly controlled by special interest. Without repealing the 17th amendment there is no stopping our welfare state beast created by liberals from both political parties.

Every day this beast is consolidating more and more power and soon states will be just designated regions. God I ask in your name, save this last bastion of true freedom in the world today, still the home of the brave, proud, and free.

OIL WELL WILD GOOSES CHASE!

Time is a wasting! I'm no oil man, and I'm no scientist, but I am a deep objective thinker. I believe time is wasting on what should have been done from the git go.

With escaping pressure around 2000 pounds per square inch over 5000 feet down only a relief well will allow a cap in my view. With that kind of pressure and that far down it is a no brainer that the pressure gotta be lowered before anything is gonna work. What do I know? We'll see, time is a wasting.

ECONOMIC UNDERSTANDING

It still amazes me of the lack of basic economic understanding that most Americans has or presumed to have.

Today I heard someone say that the tax payers won't have to foot the bill for the BP oil spill because BP make tons of profit and can well afford to pay. Hog wash, poppycock, BP don't have that kind of money, that kind of money can only come from BP raising oil prices then we all are gonna pay.

ARIZONA IMMIGRATION LAW

I'm so sick and tired of hearing supposedly intelligent people believing that this or that official hasn't read the Arizona immigration law. My God! That is one of the oldest lawyer tricks in the book.

One of the hardest things there is to get a lawyer to admit having read anything unless it is in his/her best interest. Of course, they all have read the Arizona immigration law, but you can't prove it and question someone on something they don't know anything about. Case closed.

IMMIGRATION HYPOCRITES GALORE!

I'm going to give you the cold steel or rock hard facts on immigration because no one else is going to say it out loud. The first fact is it will be impossible to solve the immigration symptom and I say symptom because the welfare state is the root problem.

All I hear is a lot of hypocritical nonsense on the subject and no one wanting to face cold hard facts. The USA can't feed itself or survive if it had to depend only on Americans to do field work and many other hard labor jobs.

Sure, I hear a lot of talk to the otherwise that is cheap, but try to tell a farmer with his harvest rotting in the field that kind of nonsense. You may not agree with me but I'll tell you how to solve the immigration problem, kick the welfare state the hell out of its super sugar daddy social and family provider role. And send it back to its designated role of collecting taxes, and protecting and defending the country.

As long as we have our existing welfare state it is futile and a waste of time and grandstanding for any politician to talk about solving the immigration symptom.

Far too many able bodied men in America don't have to work and especially doing hard labor, they can always sponge off of a mother, sister, aunt, or grandmother that is on the dole. For God sake, give me a break America.

President Ronald Wilson Reagan only had to deal with 3 millions illegals and here we are around 30 years later and around 30 millions illegals and guess what, many of the same people are still around singing the same old cop-out blues.

For God sake, give these people season work permits so they can come and go as they please and stop being hypocrites and face reality. They won't go home now because they are afraid they can't come back and work, a work permit is the only sensible thing to do.

Otherwise, they won't go home and in a few years we'll have 50 million and the same old song will still be playing and nothing will have changed as long as this welfare state has any say.

Europe doesn't have the illegal immigration problem like in the USA. The reason is they use a common sense approach like a guest worker permit.

However, something so simple and reasonable will never happen in the USA because the liberals are more interesting in gaining new voters to keep them in power than solving the problem.

WRITERS OPINION ON PUTTING ETHANOL IN GASOLINE!

I think putting ethanol in gasoline was one of the cruelest hoaxes ever pulled on the American people. Anyone that have an older or any car that is seldom driven is going to have problems.

With ethanol in it gasoline deteriorates so rapid that the gas tank needs draining after a month or so if not used. Plus, sooner or later it is going to drive the cost of all corn products out of sight.

I have an old classic car that I seldom drive and I gotta find me some ethanol free gasoline somewhere. Sometime later, shame on you Freddie Sirmans Sr, for thinking there is still individual freedom left in the USA to buy ethanol free gasoline!

Hell, how was I to know that it is mandated by the Feds that ethanol free gasoline can no longer be found in this great free country. I guess I will just have to drain all of the gas out of my old classic car and keep the tank empty or run the hell out of it. Wakeup America!
SIRMANS LOG: 12 MAY 2010, 0029 HOURS.

IS THE LIBERALS RUNNING A STALKING HORSE FOR THE UNITED STATES SUPREME COURT?

I have been wrong before and may be wrong on this. I just can't bring myself to believe that the liberals will actually vote anyone on to the United States Supreme Court that don't have a long established liberal ruling record.

In my mind it just doesn't add up, so I'm going to call the bluff and up the ante. I think they want to soften up the opposition before sending in a die hard liberal with a

long established liberal ruling record.
Remember folks, I'm just thinking out loud
here I have no reason to think this except a
gut feeling of my own. I just don't trust
liberals with power. We'll see, Maybe they
know something the rest of us don't that will
trump a long proven liberal ruling record.
However, my gut feeling is they don't and a
stalking horse strategy is being used. There
is no doubt about it, it is the roll of the dice
on the part of the liberals, who really knows
they probably hit the jackpot, but only
history will give us the proof with a proven
liberal ruling record.
**SIRMANS LOG: 10 MAY 2010, 1444
HOURS.**

MR. GOVERNMENT! PLEASE BRING BACK THE GOLD, SILVER, OR PRECIOUS METAL SELF-CONTAINED VALUE-WITHIN-ITSELF REAL MONEY

**WRITER STRESSES A POINT: 8 MAY
2010, 1453 HOURS.**
These guys on TV were talking about
spending and one made the point that
government spending money comes from
businesses and the taxpayers.
.
I agree, but, that is not the whole truth and

nothing but the truth. You want the real truth! I'll give it to you! All government income originates from some form of business profit.

.

"Profit" and nothing but profit can create wealth. When you tax choke to death the goose that lays the golden egg you go to the poor house or you starve. However, you can never get a liberal to understand that simple fact.

.

The problem with economics is not enough Americans understand it not even trained economist. The first rule is you can't separate the economy from culture and human behavior.

The next thing is using money is supposed to be only an easier means of trading and bartering, societies survived with trading and bartering long before money or a currency was invented.

Actually, the value of money is supposed to be in the money itself in the form of gold, silver, or some other precious metal, not some worthless paper backed only on faith.

It started when someone suggested why carry around all of this heavy money why not let the government print a paper note and lock the gold and silver away as a backup.

That worked just fine until the "New deal" came along and opened the door for the government to seize the traditional family provider role for itself.

Once government got a taste of the God like power of being a super sugar daddy provider the politicians went hog wild and is still spending like there is no tomorrow.

The gold backup did survive until President Richard M. Nixon just flat outright outlawed it, then the liberals from both political parties with little or no resistance found themselves in spending hog heaven and are still having a field day.

Life itself is a process of cycles and rebirths, success and failure are part of our existence and there is absolutely nothing man can do to change that fact.

That means booms, busts, good times, hard times, famines, and horrible acts of nature are always going to come around sooner or later. The only tried and true protection that has allowed man and civilization to survive over the years is to maintain and safeguard a strong culture.

A strong culture must have a strong nuclear and extended family system, a strong religious or moral code in place, and adequate backup bartering capacity, we have very little of that left.

A physical valued or gold backed currency will safe guard a nations culture by purging or holding at bay the negative anti-survival forces like moral decay, left and right extremes, and porn.

Now, the only way to save the USA is to some how rebuild her culture, but that can never happen unless the people and the states vote the welfare state beast out of its super provider role.

I knew when the liberals finally got the elderly on government health care it was going to be almost impossible to save individual freedom and America itself. Once you make people your dependents very few are going to bite the hand that feeds them.

Now, nearly 50 percent of the American people are heavily government dependent and don't pay any federal income taxes, how can you expect people to vote against their own self interest, you can't.

The nation is on a suicide mission with little

or no hope of individual freedom surviving, and even worse the young and average American still don't get it, especially the mostly liberal news media. Please God, help me educate this great nation.

This is a stress call for our survival as a free people. The big plus with getting back to a real physical currency with the value self contained within itself is it would assure survival of the people no matter how stupid the government acted.

The currency would be protected against all inflation and if you buried it or hid it under the mattress it would keep its value. Also, it would put most of the financial power back into the hands of the people.

I don't see any way USA sovereignty can be saved with the financial course we are on, the UN. or some world body will end up owning us if we don't get back to a real currency.

However, getting back to a real currency is something the people will have to demand because politicians and the government will never give up wielding their super provider God like power.

They will stop at nothing to continue trying

to do the impossible which is to keep our welfare state beast fed. There is not enough money in the whole wide world to keep financing our welfare state, but the liberals are in complete denial and are taking the great USA down for the count.

Even today if you found a buried treasure hidden by a black beard over 600 years ago its value would be just as much because the value and worth is self-container within the precious metal itself.

WRITER SHARES SOME PERSONAL EXPERIENCE!

Freedom is something the average American takes for granted. While we sleep comfortable in our cozy warm beds at night very few of us ever take time to think that vigilantly standing guard every second twenty four hours everyday protecting us is our military.

It's been a long time now nearly fifty years ago when I was active duty military and played my small part physical and up close. I have seen up close some of the might that protects us.

The old Atlas ICBM's have long been retired now, but I have been down five floors deep into the bowels of a missile silo in the

Nebraska countryside as a young U.S. Air Force firefighter.

Someone said something to this effect, "Freedom is never free."

God, I ask in your name save our great country.
SIRMANS' LOG: 18 APRIL 2010, 0944 HOURS.

THE POLITICAL DILEMMA OF A 3RD PARTY VOTE!

The thing about a 3rd party vote is there is no consolation prize it is an all of nothing game, and 99.9 percent of the time nothing is what one gets.

Everybody knows that a 3rd party movement only guarantees victory to the opposing major party, that is a given, there is no getting around that fact.

So, I say concede failure possibilities, go for broke, damn the torpedoes' full steam ahead, put it all on the line, sink or swim, it ain't over til the fat lady sings, never say never, No guts no glory is my advice to a 3rd party.

To hell with being hemmed in look what it has gotten freedom loving Americans. We have two main political parties in the USA and the only major difference is speed. One party is rushing into full socialism at warp speed and the other is crawling with a drip, drip slow motion torture into full socialism.

Sure, the liberals with their nearly 50 percent hardcore government dependents are going to win for now. But, I'm going to stake my entire God given wisdom on the fact that the American people will never accept a political system that brings undue hardship, starving, and suffering.

Individual freedom is bred into the American people and I don't believe they are going to tolerate a system like in Europe. Socialism never has and never will work it only gets worse with time.

If a 3rd party make a stand the people will come to them when they see socialism up close. That will especially be true if the two major parties keep growing government. SIRMANS' LOG: 15 APRIL 2010, 1129 HOURS.

WHY GREED CAN PREVENT MASS STARVING FROM STRIKING THE USA WITHIN 3 YEARS?

WRITERS OPINION:

Whoa, here! Let's keep our eye on the ball! Sometimes high decisions are made to placate possible lenders believing that no one wants to finance a gunslinger.

The USA has been reduced to a needy greedy financial dependent and I blame it all on our welfare state beast. It is impossible for the federal government to afford the cost of our welfare state but the liberals are in complete denial and out of touch with reality.

Nature's supreme law of "Natural selection" is now in the process of purging the whole system by letting the liberal anti-survival forces destroy almost everything. Then, out of the ruins will sprout forth a rebirth free of overpowering negative energy. But, what may rise up in a rebirth might not include individual freedom.

Otherwise, it is a long shot, but all the solutions can be found in reading Freddie L. Sirmans, Sr.'s books and writing's.
SIRMANS LOG: 7 APRIL 2010, 1429 HOURS.

WRITER'S OPINION:

When I see the liberals trying to sell the American people on the greatness of their super "Health care" victory it makes me think of a song I once heard.

Two women were competing for the same man and afterward the winner realized her big, big prize was a snake oil salesman. So, she said something to this effect, "I thought I was the best of woman but was the biggest fool!"

So, before this health care debacle is over I believe a lot more people will realize that instead of being the wisest supporters they were the biggest fools.
SIRMANS LOG: 5 APRIL 2010, 0951 HOURS.

WHY GREED CAN PREVENT MASS STARVING FROM STRIKING THE USA WITHIN 3 YEARS!!!
Misunderstanding "Greed" is the perfect example of liberals and uninformed people failing to understand human nature. It is impossible to create a wealthy nation without greed and self-interest being allowed to flourish.

Sure, like electricity greed is very dangerous and must be bridled, but it should never be shut down or restricted too severely if wealth is to be created in a nation. There is no greater or powerful energy packed motivating force in nature than greed.

That is why communism, socialism, and

every non-free market place will always fail and face mass starvation unless the nation has vast natural resources to sell or receive outside help. A million things can be tried to save the USA but I can guarantee you nothing is going to save us unless one thing is done first.

First, find people that will vote government out of its super provider role or we all perish. It is a power thing and big government as a super provider is in a race right now to finish consolidating it power for an absolute take over.

Starting with the "New deal" the people have surrendered almost all of their power to control big government except the vote, and its days are numbered, when we wake up with no individual freedom it will be too late. No one ever thought Germany would be completely taken over either.

Whoever is the provider is the ruler and in a showdown it may already be too late to prevent a complete take over. I don't make the rules I just have the wisdom to see what is actually playing out. Even a fool should be able to see what is taking place is not business as usual.

That is why if government would just get the

hell out of the way and protect the country, the free market place, and free competition, then even the poorest of the poor could pay for their own food and health care out of pocket. But, oh no, then government couldn't wield its God like power as a super sugar daddy provider.

This is so simple and has been proven to work time and time again but liberals are too shallow to see past their noses. More and more I'm beginning to believe that the liberals gaining over whelming power was a blessing in disguise.

Otherwise, no amount of trying to convince people of the dangers of liberalism could have put the fear of God in the American people like this bunch has. Except for the nearly 40 percent hardcore dependents everyone else can hardly wait to vote this bunch out.

The pendulum could swing back the other way so hard it goes off the chart. I think they want to take over everything and make peons out of everybody. I believe they are going for the jugular to kill all individual freedom in the USA.

I think they want to bust the budget for a complete out right power grab through

martial law.
SIRMANS LOG: 31 MARCH 2010, 1105
HOURS.

WHO IS REALLY THE FOOL AND NUT CASE?

Over 95 percent of the American people think
someone that thinks like me is a fool and nut
case. I have the depth and wisdom that very
few have and history will continue to prove
me right. It can take a hundred years or
longer, but there has never been and never
will be a government that didn't go broke at
some point.

History is littered with abandoned city ruins
where all of the people left due to the
economy collapsing. That is why I pound and
pound so hard of the importance of culture,
culture, and maintaining a strong nuclear
and extended family system. It should be the
responsibility of the nuclear and extended
family to pay health care cost with or without
insurance, not the government.

The same goes for keeping the homeless off
the streets, not the government except as a
last resort. What are the people going to do
when the government is broke and don't
have enough money to take care of the
people? It is very simple; there is absolutely

no way a nation can survive through hard times without a strong nuclear and extended family foundation.

Even worse in our case our welfare state beast has all but completely destroyed our culture, our nuclear and extended family system, and any capacity to barter. And this beast is protected by the liberals standing guard for it to finish the job of annihilating the USA.

The African American community is like the canary in a mine, the two parent married family will soon be something you find only in the history books.

Any reasonable intelligent person knows this economy is headed for a collapse, but don't know what the solutions are, I do. However, the most dangerous things to the survival of the USA are government red tape and mandates.

Like in California the red tape keeps the people from saving themselves, no individual or group can use initiative to save themselves without the state taking almost all of the profit. No one wants to work for nothing.

Anything that belongs to everyone in practice

belongs to no one. That is something liberals can't see. Bless their hearts, but, they should never be in charge of this nation's long term survival.

Yet, my plea for sanity is seen as this raving maniac right wing nut case that must be ignored. Sure, I agree, I'm a driven man, but it is for the survival of my country which I believe has lost its way. All of the solutions can be found in my vast writing and books. SIRMANS LOG: 29 MARCH 2010, 0941 HOURS.

THE ONLY THING MISSING NOW IS THE SECRET POLICE AND THE KNOCK IN THE MIDDLE OF THE NIGHT!!! AND THAT WILL BE NEXT!!!
HEALTH CARE PASSING MAY COLLAPSE THE USA ECONOMY AND BRING DOWN GLOBAL ECONOMY WITH IT!!!
Liberals and shallow minded people thanks raising taxes brings in more income to the government, but in reality with few exceptions it proves just the opposite. After a point more taxes just changes behavior and brings in far less revenue and we are far past that point.

With all of the new taxes and tax hikes instead of the government taking in more revenue a year from now I predict the take will be much, much less, plus there will be many more mouths to feed along with many, many more bill to pay. Give me a break, spare me.

Only a weak survival instinct and poor judgment would allow this to happen and I blame it all on our welfare state. The liberals have taken this great nation into fantasy land while good men stood by and did nothing.

I may be wrong and have been wrong many times before, still, I predict within one year after this "Big vote" passes the USA economy will have collapsed or be on the brink. I am writing these words on the eave of the "Big vote" that will determine the survival of the industrial world as we know it.

I have the exceptional God given wisdom to know beyond a shadow of doubt that the USA economy will collapse and bring the global economy down with it. I know less than five percent of the American people have the depth and wisdom to believe anything I say; still, only history can prove me wrong.

All of the answers on how to save the USA and world economy can be found in reading my books and writings. These liberals mean well and truly believe they are right but they are blind and don't know it. In reality they don't understand human nature.

Understanding human nature is something that can't be taught, it can only be learned from real or imposed hardship and struggle. A human being is not just another cog in a machine, if you take away his struggle to survive you destroy his character and make him a useless dependent, but, you can never convince a liberal of that simple fact.

They think someone like me that will only help someone that will help themselves is cruel and uncaring. America is great because great men with great wisdom made it great, not shallow minded do gooders that think doing for someone is teaching them how to survive.
SIRMANS LOG: 20 MARCH 2010, 1156 HOURS.

**THE "BIG VOTE" AFTER WORDS:
SIRMANS LOG: 21 MARCH 2010, 2257 HOURS.**
The deed is done. These good men and women in congress truly believe they have

done what is in the best interest of their country. Who truly knows, the Lord works in mysterious ways? With all of my great wisdom and judgment I totally disagree with what they have done.

I felt the same way I did when I watched the government kill the innocent Terri Schiavo. I felt like a helpless soul powerless to stop a violent crime from taking place. However, we are a nation ruled by law instead of men and I respect the law as much as anyone.

Life will go on but it will not be the same, I know I won't be the same. I believe the laws of nature that works to keep balance in the universe will use divine intervention to save individual freedom.

I believe an individual or a movement will come about and save the last bastion of true freedom left in the world today. Or course I may be wrong, but, what the heck!!??!!!???

<u>NOW ONLY THE SECOND AMENDMENT PROTECTS USA FREEDOM!!!</u>

With this complete liberal takeover of health care in the USA that means they are going for the jugular of individual freedom in

America. In almost no time all private insurance companies will be forced out of business.

All medical cost will double and you will be forced to pay or go to prison and loose everything you own. If that happens the only thing that stands between the complete lost of all individual freedom in the USA will be the second amendment, and its days will be numbered.

All of the answers that can save the USA with freedom still intact can be found in Freddie L. Sirmans, Sr's books and writings, take heed. SIRMANS' LOG: 18 MARCH 2010, 0952 HOURS.

<u>NOW CHEW ON THIS!!!</u>
PREVIEW OF USA FUTURE IF LIBERALS GET THEIR WAY!!!

Today a non free market place economy cannot exist without most of its people starving half to death. That is contrary to what the anti-capitalist ingrates think.

In past history dictators and authoritarian governments would use their armies to make weaker countries supply them with food and resources, or starve most of their own people half to death. In this modern nuclear age bulling and taking over weaker countries and living off the spoils is not going to be tolerated.

No one works extra hard and produces when someone else is sitting on their ass and receiving an equal reward. In a non free market system like that everyone tries to do the least to eat and avoid being shot.

With Fannie and Freddie gobbling up all of the real estate and their boss the federal government gobbling up banks and the automobile industry it won't be long before we citizens will be just peons.

Here is something else you can chew on, whoever are the provider rules and it sure ain't the American people anymore like it was before the "New deal."

Unless a way is found to vote the federal government out of its super sugar daddy provider role it is only a matter of time before a dictator seizes power.

However, the American voters still has the power and must stop this now because practically all politicians loves the God like power that comes with being a super sugar daddy provider and will not yield one inch.

It may already be too late with so many needy government dependents.
SIRMANS' LOG: 11 MARCH 2010, 1355 HOURS.

THE REAL REASON JOBS WENT OVERSEAS!!!

A lot of people wonder and can't understand why would our politicians send our jobs overseas? At one time they were actually subsidizing and encouraging companies to move out of the country. These are not bad people they mean well like all liberals.

Since the "New deal" liberals from both political parties have tax fed a welfare state baby into what we have now a full grown welfare state beast. And many will sell their soul, their country, and whatever they can get their hands on to keep feeding this welfare state beast.

It is very simple the liberals sent our jobs overseas in order to keep feeding our welfare state beast. Even back in the 1980's the increasing tax bite on big business was more than they could carry and stay in business, otherwise the USA economy would have collapsed in the early 1990's.

So, in order to keep feeding the welfare state

beast they knew big business must have a way to cut expenses. Politicians decided cheap labor was the way to help big business keep generating the tax money to keep their welfare state beast fed. That same thinking is what created globalization, which in my view is a fool's game.

So they greased the fast track and off went our jobs out of the country. This liberal created welfare state beast has corrupted us all too some degree how else would we keep voting the same big spenders back into office. Lord have mercy. SIRMANS' LOG: 10 MARCH 2010, 1834 HOURS.

Why demagogue the insurance companies, they don't have a gun to anyone's head making them buy, if they don't make a profit they don't survive.

When this welfare state beast forces all insurance companies out of business you are going to prison or lose everything you own if don't pay a lot more than you are paying now. Government operate on power not market forces, you'll find out!!!

ECONOMISTS CAN'T SAVE USA FROM DOOM!!!
Perspective is the reason why my great

wisdom is superior to most. I see the one leg economy in relationship to the three other legs of the four legged survival stool.

Whereas, the tunnel vision of most economists is guided by facts and figures as far as the eye can see. "Natural selection (the invisible hand)" controls an economy, in time facts and figures will always fail. The other three legs to the survival stool can be found in reading Freddie L. Sirmans' books and writings.

I am speaking with divine supernatural wisdom when I say the only way I see to save the USA as one nation with individual freedom still intact is to first abolish the minimum wage. Next, abolish almost all taxes on businesses and everything else except a very small property tax.

Third, kick the government out of its provider role by privatizing damn near everything and setup mass emergency public kitchens, shelters, and clinics, and then I'll guarantee you entrepreneurs and the free market will save this great nation intact. Of course this won't happen or even be considered.

Power always goes down with the ship and is going to take all of us down, too. Throughout history there has never been a nation that changed course knowingly headed for a crash. It may not be the type of rope it wants but at least I have thrown the nation a life line.

I know almost everyone is thinking, "Oh my God," the government needs more money not less to take care of more and more people. Wrong, that is the mentality that got this great nation in this mess.

If we could just get the government out of the free market place and its provider role it would automatically guarantee our survival, but, I'm just one lone writer ranting and raving before deaf ears, how sad.

SANTA CLAUS AND THE TOOTH FAIRY!!!

People are being told that the economy is going to recover, well, in my opinion that is like believing in Santa Claus and the tooth fairy. All government income is taken out of the profit margins of some kind of businesses or business transaction and in more and more cases not leaving enough profit for the business to survive.

.

No business can exist without making a profit. Every day local, state, and the federal government is taking in less and less revenue due to business failures, that is because of too high taxes, fees, permits, license costs, and on and on.

Instead of the government decreasing taxes and cutting spending it is doing just the opposite by hiring thousands of new employees and increasing spending by the trillions. It is not possible to get blood out of a turnip, but it seems the federal government is trying to do just that. God, I ask in your name save this great land of the free.

Come on folks, why crucify the man for letting his kids talk on the air traffic control radio. What's done is done, why take away the man's livelihood. What really need to be done is ban all kids from air traffic control towers, period. Only liberals and shallow minded people that can't take a joke would treat an innocent lack of good judgment like a murder case.

Just as Hoover couldn't stand in the way of a baby welfare state, there was absolutely no way Bunning could continue standing in the way of this full grown super welfare state beast. We are doomed!!!

All government income originates from some form of private sector excess profit, period.

There are no ifs, ands, or buts about that fact. Keeping this welfare state beast fed is the cause for us eating our seed corn and still we won't kill this beast and free ourselves.

Not only that, it has almost destroyed any means for the USA to remain a civilized nation. It has almost destroyed our nuclear and extended family system, our moral and family values (homosexual porn can't be avoided), and any emergency bartering capacity for economical survival.

And only now a few people seem to be gravely concern, mainstream media is still out to lunch. All of the answers and solutions can be found in Freddie L. Sirmans books and writing.

And another thing, true individual freedom is about common sense and thinking for yourself. Be aware, there are many false prophets today with the gift of gab that can be super charming and extremely mesmerizing with a new twist.

Cock and bull conspiracy theories are a dime a dozen, as long as one never forget to do the thinking and deciding for themselves. Freedom also means deciding if I, Freddie L. Sirmans, Sr. with all of my free advice am some type of snake oil salesman myself, I think not, you decide.

A strong nuclear and extended family system is responsible for paying for those that can't pay their own medical cost. Insurance companies don't have a gun to any one's head making them buy.

The only thing the federal government should be responsible for is paying for national defense, administrative, and a few interior cost, period; anything else is against the constitution.

Overwhelmingly the thinking is all wrong in this great country; we have lost our way and are chasing a rainbow. There is no pot of gold at the end of the rainbow, only heart ache and pain.

I think it's around 25,000 homes mortgages lost every day in the USA. Well, that tallies up to a lot of people not paying property taxes and is a big loss of revenue for local governments.

Sometimes I feel my writing is not getting traction, then I axe myself what is the alternative, to give up on saving freedom in America, me, never.

THE BIG LIE!!!

I'm so sick and tired of hearing this big lie that the bail out money avoided a depression in the USA. Hog wash, poppycock, Bull crap, or whatever, there ain't gonna be a depression in the USA because we no longer have the culture or the infrastructure to support a depression.

With the course we are on it is no longer a matter of a collapse, it's now when will it hit. With no emergency backup bartering capacity we will zip right pass a depression stage to the next stage, total chaos or some type of authoritarian rule.

All of the remedies and solutions to save the USA are found in my books and writing. You avoid a depression by getting the government the hell out of private enterprise and its super sugar daddy provider role, period. SIRMANS' LOG: 14 FEBRUARY 2010, 1543 HOURS.

THE USA IS DIGGING ITS OWN GRAVE!!!

A nation's long term survival depends on maintaining and safe-guarding a strong culture. A strong culture means having a strong nuclear and extended family system, a strong family and moral code in place, and a minimum bartering capacity.

Money as a currency is vastly more efficient than bartering, still paper money is supposed to represent a physical currency backup, and a physical currency backup is supposed to represent goods and services.

The physical currency backup link has been compromised thereby allowing a false economy to thrive. And the price for that has been the destruction of our culture and any backup capacity to barter, which is insane. Culture and bartering is civilization, you can't have one without the other.

Civilization and bartering existed long before money or a currency was invented. A nation with a strong culture and emergency backup bartering capacity can survive without money, but no amount of money can save a nation with a weak culture and no emergency backup bartering capacity.

Our welfare state beast is about to finish off destroying what's left of our culture and less than minimum bartering capacity. There are simply not enough people in the USA growing and raising their own food, and the price we are going to pay is mass starvation sooner than we think.

A nation can't have adequate emergency backup bartering capacity unless enough people have their own food to barter with. we can't keep having our cake and eating it too. There is no foreign enemy spending this country into oblivion, it is people "We" ourselves are voting into office.
SIRMANS' LOG: 11 FEBRUARY 2010, 1300 HOURS.

MY PHILOSOPHY ON ECONOMICS by Freddie L. Sirmans, Sr.
If I have to repeat it 10,000 times, "Natural selection" is what controls economics. Just like it is as equal important to be able to forget thing as it is to remember things except we never realizes it. The same applies to economics, it is just as important to have purges or busts as it is to have booms, you can't have one without the other.

The secret to everything in life is balance, even good and evil. How else is Mother Nature going to control moral decay, gross inefficiency, and over powering corruption without collapses and rebirths? Leaders of old knew this wisdom. Now, far too many people believe that big government should come in and prevent all failure, a very big mistake.

That closes off all safety valves to the

system itself and allows the negative and anti survival forces to survive and become more and more powerful until they bring down the whole system. You can't have an economy without booms and busts, it is a life cycle the way nature designed it.

Man's responsibility is to safeguard and keep a strong enough culture to survive and get through rebirths or busts whenever they occur. When small rebirths or busts occur, no problem, the problem is when the small rebirth safety valves are shut off by preventing failures like we have done, now the whole system is about to blow.

Mr. Sirmans with his great wisdom has laid out the solutions and remedies in his books and writing.
SIRMANS' LOG: 06 FEBRUARY 2010, 1013 HOURS.

IS A FINANCIAL COLLAPSE IMMINENT?
IS A FINANCIAL COLLAPSE IMMINENT?
This thing about an economic recovery and creating all kinds of make-work jobs, well, my great wisdom tells me a recovery ain't gonna happen and make-work jobs is going to hasten the collapse.

Remember, our welfare state beast feeds on more-money and every job loss means more mouths to feed with less and less tax money coming into the till.

Under this circumstance a collapse is imminent unless the federal government jettisons its super heavy social and family financial load by weaning or privatizing out of it.

It is impossible for the federal government to continue to carry this heavy financial load without collapsing. This is the belief of one lone writer, me, Freddie L. Sirmans, Sr.. I have no power to make anyone see the light.

I know I will continue to be written off as some kind of extremist right wing nut case, so be it, I mean well with good intentions. With love always.
SIRMANS' LOG: 30 JANUARY 2010, 1132 HOURS.

GOD SAVE US FROM OUR BELOVED EDUCATED FOOLS!!!
THE PARTY OF "NO" LABEL!!!
I think the party of "No" label is a badge of honor. The liberals are caught out in the

open with no one on hand to blame and hide behind.

They know the only thing that can save their hide in the 2010 election is to do what they do best, find a way to shift blame to someone else.

So, "Be aware of all Greeks bearing gifts." The tax paying voters love hearing the word "No" and is going to prove it in the 2010 election if anyone is still saying "No." SIRMANS' LOG: 29 JANUARY 2010, 1949 HOURS.

WRITER FINALLY LOSES IT!?!?
Maybe I have lost it, like the paranoid fellow that thought when the football players went into a huddle they were talking about him.

Well, for some reason when they make these "Bed wetting" remarks I keep thinking they are talking about me.

No, no, snap out of it Freddie, that's not possible. However, maybe this time I really have lost it.
SIRMANS' LOG: 27 JANUARY 2010, 0853 HOURS.

GOD SAVE US FROM OUR BELOVED EDUCATED FOOLS!!!

After the latest supreme court decision in favor of free speech for all I am in shock by the liberal reaction. My God! I didn't know how deep the hatred of big business and free enterprise had become in this great country.

I ask, where is all this flawed ignorant thinking coming from? I suspect it must be coming from our college and university systems. I thank God for our corporations, without them the USA would be worse off than most third world countries. The true problem in the USA is big government and the welfare state not big business.

Big business can't survive if it doesn't make a profit. How can you attack corporations and at the same time complain about lack of jobs if you are not ignorant. Jobs don't just drop out of heaven, who the hell do they think provide jobs if not corporations, give me a break.

I see people on TV talking about creating jobs that don't have a clue as to where jobs come from. Jobs are based on supply and demand to make a profit. Only government can create make-work jobs with you and me paying for them.

With federal, state, and local governments all taking their growing tax bite first its extremely hard for any business to make enough profit to survive let alone create more jobs. Not to mention all kinds of the license fees, permit fees, different sale taxes, and other governments mandates imposed on a business.

The fact is we have a social and family provider welfare state and there is not enough money in the whole wide world to keep feeding this beast. And we have a leadership in complete denial that won't condition the people to plant and relearn to survive like our forefathers. God save us from our beloved educated fools.

Corporations we need and love you, the common people throughout the USA like in Massachusetts are fed up.
SIRMANS' LOG: 22 JANUARY 2010, 0901 HOURS

USA LIFE BOAT!?!?!
As a writer with supernatural wisdom the only way I see to save the USA federal government is through less financial obligations, but, from arrogance it is still taking on more financial obligations, which is insane and anti survival.

To save all of the USA as one nation, wisdom dictates that we first save the federal government at all cost otherwise the USA splits into many pieces. When so much depends on government to survive the government can't just walk away, but, to fail to wean out of it is weak and irresponsible.

Here is the remedy as I see it, the federal government must jettison damn near all social and provider obligations through privatization, get rid of the minimum wage, and cut all taxes to the bone. Then the federal government will have a fighting chance to survive, otherwise only doom lies ahead.

To ignore this deep wisdom advice is to tempt fate and USA survival as one nation. That is the way it is, this ship is sinking and the federal government better take a life boat soon or go down with the ship.
SIRMANS' LOG: 23 JANUARY 2010, 0755 HOURS.

THE HAITI DEBACLE?!?!
HAITI
As a creative original thinker I've tried very hard not to comment on Haiti because I pull no punches and tell it as I see it. But, I

couldn't take it any longer I was about to pop I had to vent.

No one believes in freedom and democracy more than I do, however, there is no one thing in life that will work for every case. I seen it on TV and remember several years ago Haiti was fairly well run by their military.

The place had law and order and was a safe place for foreign investments. Several foreign factories had located there with more to come. However, there was a problem, there were reports of citizens being abused and mistreated.

Whoa, hell no, said the big giant to the north we can't have that, we must restore democracy to this sovereign state. Their military was given the boot and sent packing. Now, Haiti has been turned into a failed welfare state like the liberals has done to Michigan and are trying to do to the entire USA.

Haiti is a microcosm of what's coming to the USA if the death grip the liberals have on our great country is not broken soon. The exception being Haiti has never been a democracy and probably never will be a democracy. And in my opinion the same applies to Iraq.

PS: All of that aside now is the time to donate; I have already donated $50.00 and will be giving more and as much as my budget can stand.

* February 03, 2010 donated $25.00
* March 02, 2010 donated $25.00

"IT IS ALL OUT IN THE OPEN NOW, NOTHING ELSE TO HIDE"

"IT IS ALL OUT IN THE OPEN NOW, NOTHING ELSE TO HIDE" Right after the last election that swept in a new liberal president and super liberal majorities in both houses of congress, I said these words "It is all out in the open now, liberals will have no one else to blame, and all eyes will be on them alone."

Around eight months later after all of the "Tea Party" hype I said if voters get fed up and decide to change political horses, all you will get is a slower political team into full socialism. I still stand by that. So, to the political team now on the sideline, just hold your horses, you will be swept in in the next two elections.

Then what are you going to do? Are you going to be just a slower team into full socialism like in the past, or are you going to take down this welfare state beast set on enslaving this great predominant Christian nation, otherwise" Lead, follow, or get the hell out of the way" a third party movement will be unstoppable. **LOG ENTRY: 21 DECEMBER 2009, 1315 HOURS.**

FED UP AND DISGUSTED, I SLAM MY HAT ON THE FLOOR.
I don't care who you are if you tell me health care should be free you are ignorant, a moron, and don't understand freedom or democracy.

With your thinking that health care should be free then food, clothing, and housing should be free too there is no difference. If you have a gripe about the price, me too, the price is past the sky is the limit and somewhere out in space due to the government getting into health care in the first place.

The only way health care could be free is if the doctors, nurses, and other health care provider became slaves and cared for you free of charge. Joking aside, saying it should be free, I know that means the government should pay for it.

The people that believe that don't have a

clue as to where government income actually comes from. Like a little kid believes eggs come only from the grocery store, ninety five percent of the American people believe government income comes only from the tax payers.

Most of the money from individual tax payers and business tax payers comes out of the profit margin of the barely hanging on small business men and women of America. So, with the government demanding more and more of small business's profit, soon there won't be any successful businesses left, because no business can hire or survive unless it makes a profit.

No profit means no businesses or paid employees for the government to tax. Then all of the millions upon millions of do-for-me government dependents our liberal welfare state beast has produced will be rioting in the streets and at each others throats. **LOG ENTRY: 13 DECEMBER 2009, 0055 HOURS**

BRIEFLY BACK TO THE STONE AGE LECTURE. Through out my writing I have mention civilization going back to the Stone Age and for that a lot of people think I'm crazy and ignorant.

That is because so few understand basic economics. Basic economics starts with the individual nuclear and extended family system then leads on to a community bartering system.

However, bartering is an extremely limited economic system because no one may want what you have to offer and then you are stuck. Gold, silver, or some other rare precious metal used as a currency solved the extremely limited bartering problem.

Still, the value of a physical currency is in the currency itself no matter who has it. A government can't manipulate and devalue a physical currency when the value is in the currency itself, or print up and handout money it don't have.

Fast forward to today, the welfare state with its unlimited capacity to tax and print worthless paper money has almost destroyed our nuclear and extended family system along with any capacity to barter. And without these basic foundation building blocks no society can survive through hard times, it is impossible.

Folks, I will sum up by saying, I'm just a lone writer doing my thing, and telling it as I see it. I have a fifty fifty or one out of two chance of being right. Besides, who listens to me, a whole lot of people think I'm a kook and off my rocker anyway.

There really is no guaranteed individual wealth anymore. If you bury or hide money under the mattress today next week there may be a whole new world currency. Also, no individual truly owns property anymore with the cost of property taxes and it may be twice as much next year.

Get a grip people; you better use your vote sensible and vote out these big progressive liberal spenders while you still can. Love you, and thanks for reading my work, God bless. **LOG ENTRY: 08 DECEMBER 2009, 1O12 HOURS.**

THE BIG TRIAL IN NEW YORK CITY.
Let me throw my two cent worth in here. In my mind there is no limit to how shallow liberals can be. Protect New York City from what! Sure the trial is going to go on and definitely will be protected.

But, it is the roll of the dice and is opening up a can of worms. Can New York City protect every store, hotel, mall, rail road, and on and on like in Tel Aviv. Why invite the unknown, lets just hope my extreme caution is just pesky nonsense.

MINIMUM WAGE:

A minimum wage is like a vehicle with no reverse or an army walled of from any retreat. Getting rid of the minimum wage and cutting taxes to the bone will at least save the USA from total chaos and allow us to live and fight another day.

Where do most citizen tax payers get their money, from their small business employers? Where do businesses get their money, from citizen customers, some of which they themselves employ. As you can see the economy operates as a giant cycle.

Human energy and intelligence creating something of value in the form of food and resources is what keeps this cycle going. And the rewarding byproduct of the whole process is what's called profit. That is what government takes, all taxes ultimately comes from some form of profit.

Sure, government needs a certain amount of profit driven tax money to protect the nation from both foreign and domestic enemies and basic interior needs. But, the USA government was never designed to be a cradle to grave social and family provider.

Now, big government at all levels is taking far too much of small businesses profit for many of them to survive let alone hire anyone. And you gonna tell me mass tax cuts to the bone is not the answer, go fly a kite!!!

STONE AGE.
Most people with common sense think the biggest threat to the survival of the USA is its financial crisis cause by big government spending. I don't think so, I think what is slowly driving the dagger in the heart of this great nation is what big government has done to our nuclear and extended family system.

No famine, financial collapse, nuclear attack, mass chemical attack, or mass biological attack can destroy this huge nation with our strong nuclear and extended family system along with our minimum bartering capacity, is this statement true or false? Then you be the judge.

In terms of raw survival big government as the welfare state has destroyed everything and left us with a leadership in complete denial along with countless gimmy, gimmy, do for me dependents. Culture and survival wise just about the only option we have left is to regress back to the Stone Age unless our leaders snap out of denial and face cold steel rock hard reality.

Folks, I'm just a lowly lone writer telling it as I see it, pray that I'm wrong. Like a broken record I repeat, no one wants this but it would keep us from going back to the Stone Age. Get rid of the minimum WAGE and cut taxes to the bone across the board.

Then whatever income the government takes in should first go to national defense and administrative cost, and whatever is left go to community kitchens, hospitals, and shelters. Sure, its extreme but it is better than going back to the Stone Age. If anyone has a better solution they better step up now because I see the Stone Age over the horizon.

Everybody is all worked up over health care and socialism. But, unless my advice to get rid of the minimum wage and cut taxes to the bone is taken serious nothing is going to stop the USA and global economy from going back to the Stone Age.

Cost, cost, and more cost is the problem with health care and if the government thinks it can take it over and not pay the cost it will destroy medical care in America. However, it is going to take it over anyway if not today it will be tomorrow, because the only way to stop it would be to dismantle the welfare state and I'll leave it at that.

And the root reason why medical cost has shot through the roof pass the sky is the limit into outer space is because government got into it in the first place. Anything the government gets into in a free country the cost will always go through the roof because government doesn't adhere to market force principals. Enough said.

As to capitalism versus socialism that is the least of our problems. No form of government can save a nation from doom if it looses its nuclear and extended family foundation, which we have. I know I keep writing the same thing over and over but if I can enlighten just one mover and shaker it will be worth it. Amen.

HELPFUL HINT: 23 OCTOBER 2009, 1421 HOURS.
This is when one desperately needs to stay awake because life, property, or job may be on the line.
Technique: Hold any small object such as a

quarter, house keys, car keys, etc. in your hand, if you start to doze off it will drop and when it hits the floor you will snap awake every time, just don't forget to pick it up. *This technique is not design for anyone driving a vehicle.

LATE ENTRY III: 20 OCTOBER 2009, 1335 HOURS.
IS IT DESTINY OR FROM A HIGHER POWER?
I, Freddie L. Sirmans, Sr. a shy neurotic uneducated south Georgia USA country boy is now teaching the world basic economics, somebody need to teach it. Ninety nine percent of the American people don't know what is actually powering this big USA and global economic ship.

Without this source power the whole USA and global economy will be left adrift. Almost everyone thinks its power comes from the government and the American tax payers. That is a source but it is not the root source, plus almost all thinking stops there.

Very few probe deeper and discovers who is actually paying taxes to the government. And even those that do acknowledge that it is the business and working people of America, and that is the end of it.

American small businesses do employ far more people in this country than anything else so that must be the main source powering the USA economy. Well, I guess that's it we have an open and shut case.

Whoa, not so fast, I beg the difference, for the record I will prove that it is something called "Profit" that is the root source that powers the USA economy or any successful economy. We all need a certain amount of food and basic resources to live on. So, whatever amount over what we need to survive on is what's called extra or profit that we can exchange for money or whatever.

The accumulation of excess profit is what makes one rich or wealthy. A business is only a medium to exchange goods or services for a profit, no profit, no business, no employee, and nothing for the government to tax. Big government at all levels, federal, state, and local has put so many taxes, license fees, permit fees, rules, regulations, and other mandates on a business that it is a miracle anyone makes a profit.

Almost any blood sucking economic system will work for 80-100 years, then its hell to pay. This welfare state system is like a dog chasing its tail because a business is only a means of exchange; all cost must be passed on to the public which in turn raises the cost of living on everyone. I rest my case your honor.

The USA economy is now at the point it fits the old proverbial saying: "A straw broke the camels back."

LATE ENTRY II: 14 OCTOBER 2009, 0831 HOURS.
I once heard this story about a man with a mule that would walk about twenty yards or so stop briefly and continue on and on. Someone asked the owner what was the problem with this mule, why he acted like that?

The owner said the mule was afraid he might not hear the owners command so he stops to listen. Well, I think that same analogy can be applied to the liberals running this country.

They have all of the power and are almost totally in control of this great country. So, what is the problem with them, why are they acting the way they are? I ask why don't they just follow their own beliefs and convictions and stop all of this stopping for bipartisan support.

The fact is: The idea of taking on

responsibility all alone with no one else on hand to shift blame to, scares the hell out of a liberal.

LATE ENTRY: 10 OCTOBER 2009, 1016 HOURS

The financial burden load of the welfare state has bankrupted this nation and sent our manufacturing and jobs over seas. But, that is not the worst thing the welfare state beast has done to this great predominate Christian nation.

The worst thing is it has ripped out the inner fabric of this great nation by destroying our nuclear and extended family system, and any capacity to barter, there is no recovery from this, Stone Age here we come. However, the future is never written in stone. Getting rid of the minimum wage and cutting taxes to the bone can still save us.

Getting rid of the minimum wage and cutting taxes to the bone, you must be crazy, of course that's not going to happen, the power structure and big money will go down in flames first. If only enough common sense citizens would pledge to vote for people willing to get rid of the minimum wage and cut taxes to the bone this great predominate Christian nation would be saved.

* There is an old saying that: "If you say something long enough and loud enough eventually someone is going to believe you." Maybe not mine but some nation is going to believe me.

Draft fear and the liberal media was really what caused the lost in Vietnam. Even General Giap himself admitted something to that of fact when he said only the America media gave them the hope to fight on.

With bombing accuracy and other high technology US military advantages are ten times greater than back then.

"Quitters don't win and winners don't quit." Just an opinion by writer, Freddie L. Sirmans, Sr. 4 October 2009, 0951 Hours.

FREDDIE L. SIRMANS, SR'S LOG: 14 SEPTEMBER 2009, 1231 HOURS. RECOVERY, RECOVERY, BS! My God! My God! Come on folks, economics ain't rocket science; a hundred and fifty years ago almost everyone knew what I keep telling people. It is not just the shallow minded liberals, hardly anyone anymore have a strong survival instinct.

Anyone that thinks the USA can continue to carry the financial burdens of our big government welfare state is either in complete denial or just plain ignorant. If you think I am a fool and nut case, you are wrong.

History has proven that it is always the masses that are wrong. I have the wisdom and survival instinct to know beyond a shadow of a doubt that I'm right, so help me God. However, reason never changes closed minds.

Very few people truly understand how an economy works as well as I do. Almost everyone think in term of big money, but it is not the amount it is the buying power that counts in the long run.

The other team can't run up the score if you got the ball. It is the same in economically terms; prices can't go above what the always larger poorer population can afford to pay. That is unless a big government welfare state unconstitutionally hands out free money on an individual basis.

That act subsidizes high prices, and is what

feeds this never ending inflationary spiral that we are caught up in. Sure, you can help the poor, but you can't hand out cash and food stamps on an individual basis and not destroy the free market place price structure.

That is because there is just two teams the seller (merchants) and the Buyer (consumers). And the government is supposed to fill the role of referee and tax collector. However, that is no longer the case the government is taking tax money from one team and giving it to the other.

Mother Nature says hell no, that breaks nature's supreme law of "Natural selection;" and she is preparing to step in and create a rebirth by starving the whole system back to the Stone Age.

If the government was not hogging the free market place, the free market place would heal itself. Now, the only way to get this beast out of the market place is to starve it out, it has grown far too powerful. Otherwise, there is no way to keep the USA from starving to death in just a very few years, you mark my word.

In my view the USA and the global economy is in a state of mass denial. No one wants to face the cold steel rock hard reality. If I have to repeat it a thousand times, man cannot use figures and intelligence to manage a successful economy because the variables are infinite.

However, there is nothing complicated or secret about how to run a time tested successful economy. There is a proven time tested ideology that has never failed to produce far more food and goods than any one nation can consume.

That ideology is, "Allow free competition and let the free market work," it is just that simple. But no, today we have all of these learned economists that think they can out smart Mother Nature, wrong. It is like having a vehicle with no reverse, you can't have a free floating free market place economy with a minimum wage.

You can't have a lasting free market place economy when sky high taxes and every other kind of government mandate is siphoning off most of a business's profit. For a democracy to survive and last every individual and family unit must carry its own weight. I keep hearing about a recovery, that is BULLSHIT!

I can only speak for my self, but in my view it is impossible to have a recovery with all of the financial burdens our welfare state is now carrying, after years of adding more and more the load is just too much. Also, I believe unless the minimum wage is junked and taxes cut to the bone more and more businesses are going to fail with even higher unemployment.

Listen up! Profit, profit, profit, is everything; there will be nothing for the government to survive on itself if not enough business's is making enough profit to stay afloat.

The government can only tax a profitable business, no one making a profit, nothing for the government to tax because not even Joe public gets paid if he doesn't have a job, it's just that simple. Think about it.

According to the constitution the only financial burdens our federal government should be carrying is to protect the nation from foreign and domestic enemies and to finance a healthy interior department.

But, oh no, we gave the "New deal" a foot in the door and since then liberal politicians from both parties have created this welfare state beast that is determine to grab absolute power and take away our individual freedom.

I say hell no! This beast has taken on financial burdens galore even as small as a hangnail, all out of the hard earned profits of the barely hanging on large and small business men/women of America. I say, snap out of it learned economists, face reality; lets take our bitter medicine and go boldly into the future.

We can do all things through God which strengthens us, Phil. 4-13 paraphrased.

UNDERSTANDING INFLATION!
FREDDIE L. SIRMANS, SR'S LOG: 07 SEPTEMBER 2009, 1552 HOURS UNDERSTANDING INFLATION!
In my view there is a big difference between the excessive printing of money inflation and the true cost of living inflation. I don't think very many people including economists understand what causes and drives true cost of living inflation, I do, and nuggets of it is found throughout my writing.

Printing a lot of worthless money alone can't drive the cost of living up. Government spending alone can't drive the cost of living up. Government can spend and build like crazy and that alone still won't drive the cost of living up.

There is only one way to drive the cost of living up on everyone, government consumer price support, there is simply no other way it can be done that I can see. An economy consists of only two players, the merchant and the consumer.

The process of "Natural selection" will always maintain a natural balance between the two. That is what controls and runs every economy. Sure, man can tinker and fiddler around with it but sooner or later the process of "Natural select" is going to complete a rebirth cycle. And the smartest thing man can do is maintain and safeguard a strong enough culture to survive a collapse or rebirth.

When the government gives masses of people on an individual basis enough money to pay whatever the merchant demands that is what drives inflation. Every penny the government takes comes out of the profit margin of some business or service if traced back far enough.

So, the more government takes the higher price the business will have to charge consumers to make a profit, or go out of business. That is what sets up the cost of living inflationary spiral that forces government to keep raising taxes higher and higher to give its masses of dependents enough money to support higher and higher merchant prices in a never ending spiral.

The truth of the whole matter is I can't see how the USA economy can last very much longer as a social and family provider. I can only hopes and pray for a miracle because that is what it is going to take to save the USA as one nation.

TEA PARTIES AND TOWN HALL MEETINGS ARE A WASTE OF TIME.
FREDDIE L. SIRMANS, SR'S LOG: 1 SEPTEMBER 2009, 2247 HOURS.
TEA PARTIES AND TOWN HALL MEETINGS ARE A WASTE OF TIME.

I don't enjoy raining on anyone's parade; I'm just writing what I think and believe, please forgive me. In my view the tea parties and town hall meetings is a lot of ado but lacking in problem solving. The first question I ask is what do anyone involved expect to result after all of the effort.

If someone can give me just one problem that will be solved after all of the effort I will gladly eat crow and backpedal. What is the focus? You can't solve a problem if you don't focus on it. When a predator goes after a prey meal he/she doesn't go after the whole herd, no, just one is focused upon, otherwise it is wasted effort.

Let's just say that after all of the tea party excitement is over, the voting public throws one political party out and change horses. All you will get is a slower team. The welfare state beast will still be consolidating more and more power for the eventually take over. However, I am so proud of the decent caring Americans trying to take back their country; maybe I am wrong on this. I hope so.

The only way I see our individual freedom is going to be saved is for the people and the states to take back control over the federal government. And that can only be done by starving this beast out of its all powerful social and family provider role, which the American voters are not prepared to do. We might as well accept our sad fate. I know deep in my heart that only a miracle can save the last great bastion of true freedom in the world today.

My take is the welfare state beast is biding its time. It knows it is firmly in control as the great super family provider with millions upon millions of dependents that is not going to bite the hand that feeds them. However, the American voting public still has the power to take back control of the federal government for themselves but don't know how.

Even worse the voting public doesn't have the will to take back control even if they did know how. That said, I will tell you how to take back control of your government. Focus on voting in office only people that is willing to "get rid of the minimum wage and cut taxes to the bone."

That is the only way to stop the welfare state beast from carrying out a complete take over of the USA. It is either the beast or us freedom loving Americans, there is no middle ground. If the American people are not willing to take down this beast by starving it out of its super family provider role, then no amount of tea parting or anything else is going to save individual freedom in America.

The founding fathers creation has been flipped upside down. Now, the federal government is the boss and has the power, and we the people and the states are almost powerless dependents that only have the vote. And the states don't even have 2 votes anymore because senators are no longer appointed by state legislatures.

And, we the people won't have the vote much longer unless we vote in people that will junk the minimum wage and cut taxes to the bone. That will starve this beast out of its all powerful family provider role. This nation was designed for the power to reside with the people and the states with the federal government filling the dependency role. I rest my case your honor.

Note: The USA junking the minimum wage and cutting taxes to the bone may put a stop to the spread of nuclear weapons as a byproduct, just a passing thought.

PS: Most people think I don't care about the desires and needs of the people, wrong. Sure, I care deeply, but my focus is so much, much bigger, it is about the sheer survival of my homeland as one nation with individual freedom still intact.

Most people don't believe the dire threats I keep talking about even exist. But, I have been blessed with the wisdom to know that it is real. I have already stated the only solution. Thank you God for my life health and strength. Amen.

IS A PERPETUAL MOTION ENGINE

POSSIBLE?

FREDDIE L. SIRMANS, SR'S LOG: 12 AUGUST 2009, 1821 HOURS

IS A PERPETUAL MOTION ENGINE POSSIBLE?

The idea of a perpetual motion engine has been around probably as long as engines been around. Inventors have used compressed air, battery power, and anything you can think of trying to keep an engine running almost forever.

All for naught, the idea is an illusion. But, there are still people around today that think it's possible. It is the same way with an economy. There are still far too many people around today that think you can forever run an economy without a rebirth.

The facts are the same, it is all an illusion, and it can't be done. In economic survival terms stocks, bonds, and everything done on Wall Street is an illusion and side issue. No portfolio means anything if money has no value.

And even if money has value it means nothing if you have no food to eat or if those that have food won't sell. As I have said many times in terms of raw survival money are way down the list, people survived long before money was invented. In terms of long time survival culture is far more important than money.

No amount of money can save a nation when everyone is at each others throat. If the USA culture was strong and healthy far more people would agree with me and realize the only way to save the USA is to junk the minimum wage and cut taxes to the bone.

I can only hope I'm wrong, because I believe when we starts starving in mass numbers it will be because no one can start small and grow. It will be because the minimum wage and sky high taxes won't let entrepreneurs feed themselves and the nation.

Rich people are not the same as poor people with money, there is a world of difference in motivation and mentality. Lottery winners have proven that fact. When have any lottery winner ever built a financial empire that employed a hundred thousand people.

Socialism and communism fails because there are no entrepreneurs. And there are no entrepreneurs because there is no extra reward given for extra effort. Everybody tries to give the least amount of effort to survive.

No one in America have ever had to live in a

system like that, we all need to be counting our blessings. Sure, everyone will be equal, but equal poor. I say, hell no!

Economic lecture #12
by Freddie L. Sirmans, Sr.
High drama, stay tuned for next episode.

PS: I believe this "Bed wetting thing" is some kind of inside joke, because I don't get it.

THE LAST USA LIFELINE, TAKE IT!!!
FREDDIE L. SIRMANS, SR'S LOG: 06 AUGUST 2009, 0913 HOURS
THE LAST USA LIFELINE, TAKE IT!!!
If the USA is to survive two things must be done now, otherwise I, Freddie L. Sirmans, Sr. can't see this great country surviving as one. Huh, who the hell are you, whoa, hold your horses, I'm just one lonely writer exercising my right of free speech while I still can, I don't expect to be taken seriously.

But, I am as deadly serious as a heart attack. The two must things: Junk the minimum wage and cut taxes to the bone immediately. The variables are just too numerous ONLY WHAT I JUST SAID WILL SAVE US from chaos and the total breakdown of western civilization, maybe even back to the stone age.

What happen to living off the land? Actually food and water can be free it is the piping and shipping that cost. High taxes and the minimum wage are going to be the bane that starves western civilization back to the Stone Age. It is better to work only for food and eat than it is to starve to death, in time a minimum wage places starving above eating.

You mark my word, very soon when this global economy starts unraveling there won't be anything left to do but starve because no one will be able to start small. Blocking almost all initiative will be the minimum wage and sky high taxes causing millions upon millions to starve NEEDLESSLY.

ONLY A MIRACLE CAN SAVE THE USA AS ONE NATION.
FREDDIE L. SIRMANS, SR'S LOG: 30 JULY 2009, 1350 HOURS.
ONLY A MIRACLE CAN SAVE THE USA AS ONE NATION.

I truly believe that only a miracle can save the USA as one nation. However, I do believe in miracles. It is sad for me to say but I believe it is only a matter of time before the liberals actually get their long awaited one payer medical care system. That doesn't mean anti big government opponents like me should just roll over.

When I look at the big battle going on, on capital hill about overhauling our medical care system it is no secret that the liberal's ultimate goal is socialized medicine. In my view its not going to matter a whole lot what they do because runaway medical cost can't be fixed until first the economy is fixed. And our economy can't be fixed until our welfare state beast is starved out of existence.

Yes, I said it, we must get rid of our welfare state, but I doubt you can find even 5 percent of the USA population that will agree with me on doing that. If you go back over 5 thousand years of written history there has never been any form of government like a welfare state until the "New Deal" came along.

The nuclear and extended family, the church, and social organizations have always taken care of the poor, homeless, and downtrodden, but never a government until western civilization followed the "New Deal" suit. Wise men of old had the wisdom to realize no matter what happens, don't ever destroy your lifeblood nuclear and extended family system by removing a survival need for it.

That is the one thing no civilization can recover from, that is why I cry and plead so hard for even an ounce of sanity. And I have over 5 thousand years of proof backing me up. The nuclear and extended family is the support and building block foundation of every society known to man, there are no exceptions.

Cutting taxes to the bone thereby creating a survival need for it is the only way to bring back the strong nuclear and extended family system that will save this great land of the free and home of the brave. Our welfare state is a provider form of government and that alone makes it the boss, dependents, you best mind your manners.

Like the saying goes, you can't have two captains of the same ship and sooner or later individual freedom is not going to survive with government as a social and family provider. It is already beginning to happen. Today the welfare state has created too many dependents that believe only in bigger and more government, so, now it is only a matter of when, not will the economy collapse.

I don't like admitting it, but the odds are in favor of the liberals eventually getting everything they want, thereby destroying the USA for good in the process. The "New Deal and its programs allowed the camel to get it's nose under the tent, then flamboyant liberals using The gift of gab and The course of least resistant" sunk this country to where it is today.

Nature's law of "Taking the course of least resistance" affects us all too some degree and there is no getting around that fact. And the liberals are experts at "Taking the course of least resistance" and shifting blame, which in most cases is not the wisest course to take. The welfare state beast we have today is the result of mostly liberal thinking and spending money we don't have.

There is no doubt in my mind that individual freedom in the USA will not survive as long as our welfare state is in power. Nothing and I mean nothing is going to prevent it from eventually consolidating to absolute take over power, unless its money supply power source is taken away. That means this beast must be starved to death if individual freedom is to survive in the USA.

There is no other way; it is now either it or us who love individual freedom. To hell with the shallow minded liberals, they sold out over 80 years ago with the "New Deal" and have been selling the country down the river ever since. "Long live my homeland, the home I love."

I'LL TAX YOU, TAX YOU, AND TAX YOU, TO KINGDOM COME.
FREDDIE L. SIRMANS, SR'S LOG: 20 JULY 2009, 2051 HOURS

I'LL TAX YOU, TAX YOU, AND TAX YOU, TO KINGDOM COME.
All big tax and spenders are not liberals but there is no doubt they are the ones leading the herd. I'll go even farther and say that most of the people that are for higher and higher taxes are shallow and selfish. They lack the perspective and depth to understand cause and effect.

Liberals can't see the human factory in dealing with people; they think when you tax the hell out of a person it ends there. They don't understand the relativity effect. They either don't understand or don't care that when you raise taxes it always changes behavior, what is that if not selfish.

They don't understand that today even the middle income folks has to spend every red cent trying too keeping up. They don't understand the money the government is taking and squandering is not kept in that person's community providing a livelihood for some hard working soul.

Liberals think someone like me is mean, cold, and uncaring, wrong. They think someone like me is against helping the poor, wrong. I'm against conditioning the poor to be a dependent. The liberals have it backward with helping the poor.

The liberals believe in helping the poor first and then begging them to help themselves, whereas I believe in forcing the poor to try to help themselves first then I'll give the shirt off my back to someone genuine trying to survive. I understand why the liberal media and others see someone like me as uncaring and out of touch.

That is because they have never paid a severe price for survival. Throughout history almost nothing of any true lasting value has come about without some type of great struggle. Almost my whole existence has been and is still about a severe mental struggle to survive with pride and dignity.

No one has to tell me how it feels to be ridiculed, laughed at, humiliated, and counted out even to the extreme. I have experienced and know what severe self-hate and self-shame feels like, and you tell me I don't care and has no feeling for the down trodden, yet, I have survived and am still standing.

No one can convince me I have an excuse for failure. I know personally that to try and keep trying works. I know the true power of forgiveness, or I wouldn't be still standing. Please excuse me for a little self-serving on speaking about me personally but sometimes things just need to be said.

The thing about survival is there are things no one can see or understand unless they personally pay the price. That is why destiny has brought me, Freddie L. Sirmans, Sr's out of the wood works to sound the alarm. I may seemingly be unqualified, uneducated, neurotic, and counted out but sounding the alarm must go forth, regardless.

22 JULY 2009, 1315 HOURS, ADD ON.
The United States of America has been around over 200 years and in my opinion its survival is under the gravest threats ever. But, very few people know what the gravest threat of all is or even have the wisdom to believe it when told.

There is no sense in me beating around the bush building up suspense. "Too many people believing more government is the answer" is in my view the gravest of all threats this great country ever faced.

When you go back before the "New deal" when this "More government mentality" first got a foot in the door around 80 years ago, then it was the nuclear and extended family system that kept the hungry fed and the homeless off the streets. Since then it's been all down hill ever since. There is no sense in me going on and on trying to convince shallow minds.

I'll sum it up by saying unless taxes are cut to the bone across the board to bring back a survival need for the nuclear and extended family system there will be no saving the USA as one nation. I may not be right about a lot of things but there is no doubt that I'm right on this.

If my wisdom is ignored it really won't matter what other actions are taken the USA as we know it will not survive. There has never been and never will be a society that survived long term without a healthy nuclear and extended family system, "You can look it up." God I ask in your name save my homeland.

22 JULY 2009, 1829 HOURS, 2ND ADD ON.

No form of government is going to succeed without an adequate nuclear and extended family system foundation in place. A lot of people are concerned about this nation going completely socialist when it looks like the government is trying to seize absolute power.

Well, my take on this whole scenario is, dealing with a depression or going socialist would be a cakewalk to what I believe we are about to face. I believe the USA and western civilization is about to face chaos and the total breakdown of society when this global economy fails.

I base this on the fact that the welfare state system has almost completely destroyed the fabric that holds any society together. The things I'm talking about are an adequate nuclear and extended family system, an adequate moral and family value system, and an adequate emergency backup bartering capacity.

We as a nation have very little of any of those survival tools left. This is something I have been yelling about for years, still, ain't nobody listening, how sad.

24 JULY 2009, 0834 HOURS, 3RD ADD ON.

I see where the minimum wage is going up again. I am against any minimum wage so you know up front where I stand on the issue. Next to the welfare state I believe the minimum wage is the second most destructive thing that has been done to free enterprise in America and Western Europe.

It is like General motors building a vehicle with no reverse, which of course no one would buy. You can't have success without failure. You can't have progress without mistakes. You can't grow big without starting small. The higher the minimum wage the harder it is to start at all. We can't survive with no one providing any jobs.

The problem is very few people including economist truly understand the foundation of economics. Almost everyone thinks cutting taxes to the bone will destroy the USA, wrong. Sure, it would be a nightmare and would destroy wealth as we know it along with all of the crud, inefficiency, moral decay, and everything else choking this country to death.

But, out of the rebirth would spring forth more greatness than ever before; otherwise the course of higher and higher taxes we are on is guaranteed doom.

The liberals for many years have been slowly tightening the screws closing off all common sense and it's now beginning to come to a head. I have said many times it is not the amount of dollars that matters; it is really the buying power of the dollar that matters.

A million dollars is not going to keep you alive if there is no food to buy or if those that have it won't sell. No amount of modern technology or materialistic creature comfort is going to matter if you don't have food to eat.

So, when you see all of this reckless printing of worthless money that is promoting a farther culture decline, it is only a matter of time before starvation raises it ugly head. Food and culture goes hand in hand and our culture is almost gone, lack of food will soon follow, whether you believe me or not. I rest my case.

A SUPER GREAT BRAIN STORMING

HEALTH CARE IDEA!

FREDDIE L. SIRMANS, SR'S LOG: 19 JULY 2009, 1155 HOURS.

A SUPER GREAT BRAIN STORMING HEALTH CARE IDEA!
This may sound radical and surprising coming from a die hard anti-big government advocate like me. Seriously, do Americans really want health care fixed or not. Well, I'll tell you how, you may not agree or like it but it's the most safe and practical approach to our life or death health care problem that I've ever heard of.

First, responsible leadership should set up in several large cities a test system similar to the veterans system, but, keep it separate by using only a token like script. Next, issue the scrip to only those below a certain income or other qualifying conditions.

After about a year or so there should be some proven results one way or another, that way we may not destroy the best health care system to ever exist in the history of mankind. Note, I didn't say the cheapest, but it is by far the best in the world. If test results are positive, sure, it could be expanded.

Still, my belief is the only way to save the USA medical health care system or even the economy itself is to kick the government completely out of it, period. If the government insist on being uncle sugar then fund public only things off to the side, but don't destroy the nation's culture, economy, and everything else in the process.

When government is out of the way natural selection market forces will never let prices or anything else get out of control. "You can't get blood out of a turnip and a chain is only as strong as its weakest link." A business can't charge more than the poor can pay, that is if the government butt out mind its own business and let the nuclear family fulfill its proper role.

THE MYTH OF FREE HEALTH CARE!
FREDDIE L. SIRMANS, SR'S LOG: 08 JULY 2009, 1320 HOURS.
THE MYTH OF FREE HEALTH CARE!
I really don't know where to start on this subject because so few have the perspective to see the big picture on this matter.
Anyway, I'll just start with research and who brought modern medicine to the high level it is today. You better believe it was not a one payer communist or socialist system.

It is what's left of the good ole private enterprise free market system in the USA and its research that blazes the way in modern medicine. And another thing, big government has created this "Do for me" dependency mentality so strong that most people see the medical insurance companies as the big bad boogie man, not true, but they are guilty of paying the wrong people.

There should be a law forbidding the insurance companies from paying anyone other than who takes out the insurance that would solve ninety nine percent of the insurance blame game politics. Sure, there would be a trust factor, but the patient would always know what is coming out of his hide and it would control care giver greed.

Medical care and medical insurance should be two entirely different things with one not influencing the other. Let's brain storm and leave medical insurance out of the picture for a moment. Okay, you go to the doctor and he treats you and charges you a fee. He will expect you to pay the whole fee or as much as possible at the time.

Most people won't have the lump sum or it will cause them a severe hardship, this is where medical insurance companies found a niche. Without insurance or government involved market forces would definitely control prices. That is the true problem in the medical profession today there is no market forces to help control prices, just like throughout the economy.

What people forget is medical insurance like all businesses is profit driven. For insurance companies to survive they can only insure healthy people and hope too many won't become sick at one time. However, today most people have come to see insurance companies as a cash cow just like big government.

The doctors, nurses, and other medical workers can't work for free for you to have free health care like some have come to expect, they have to eat pay high taxes and live, too.

HOW IT WAS <u>BEFORE GOVERNMENT GOT INVOLVED IN HEALTH CARE</u>

<u>6 WORDS WILL DETERMINE IF USA SURVIVES OR GOES THE WAY OF THE ROMAN EMPIRE.</u>
FREDDIE L. SIRMANS, SR'S LOG: 03 JULY 2009, 1013 HOURS

In 6 words I will tell you why the USA can be saved and not go the way of the Roman Empire. The 6 words are "The government shouldn't be a Provider." Sure, only on a temporary basis during an emergency the government must come to the aid of its people.

Today Very few people know what wealth is and how it is created, that is why most of the world is poor and will always be poor. Liberals have never understood wealth and still don't to this day, that is why only a miracle will save the USA with liberals in almost total control.

Wealth is the result of excess human energy in some form, that will be a foreign language to most that reads this, but it's true. A nuclear family, a state, and a nation all is made up of individuals. And in the final analysis that is the main thing that determines the health and wealth of any nation.

No sane individual is going to produce anything extra when the government takes it away and doles it out to non producers no matter the reason. Government is a destroyer of wealth and incentive; only private enterprise will produce more than enough food and wealth for the individual and the nation. Sure, some nations can prosper by selling natural resources but that is not producing and creating wealth.

What belongs to everyone in reality belongs to no one, and no caretaking will take place except by force. Whereas, there is no greater excess wealth producing forces on earth than greed and self-interest. Greed and self-interest should be bridled and harnessed but never, never completely shut down like in communist and socialist governments.

Only individual freedom and a private enterprise free market system will allow two of the most powerful motivating forces on earth greed and self-interest to generate more excess energy in wealth than you can shake a stick at. Sure, like electricity greed and self-interest can be very dangerous but they are not your enemy.

INDUSTRIALIZED WORLD DEPENDS ON USA GOVERNMENT SURVIVAL
FREDDIE L. SIRMANS, SR'S LOG: 01 JULY 2009, 1700 HOURS
OUR LIBERAL WELFARE STATE BEAST WILL NEVER ACCEPT GUNS IN THE HANDS OF PRIVATE CITIZENS. MY

<u>GUESS IS VERY SOON THE RIGHT FLANK WILL BE ATTACKED USING SOME TYPE OF REGISTRATION DISGUISE.</u>

FREDDIE L. SIRMANS, SR'S LOG: 14 JUNE 2009, 0730 HOURS
WORLD DEPENDS ON USA GOVERNMENT SURVIVAL!
LECTURE #5 ON USA ECONOMY
Even before I became a self-made author I was preaching against big intrusive government. I have since coined our big government a welfare state beast. To the shallow it may seem like I am against all government, wrong, nothing could be further from the truth. I actually love good government, but I view big intrusive government as a threat to individual freedom.

Government is the foundation of civilization and no organized society can survive without some type of government. Today I believe the hope and survival of the whole industrialized world depends on the USA government being saved.

The USA government and the USA people are supposed to be two difference things. But today, in a sense big government spending has placed us in the same boat and tied with the same financial burdens. From the beginning when the Continental Army won our freedom from England the USA has never known anything besides individual freedom along with a free market place.

Then along came the "New deal" and the growing of big government started smothering individual freedom and our free market place. Today, after eighty years the last of our individual freedom along with our free market place is under seize by a monster size welfare state beast.

How we deal with the key word "Financial-burdens" will determine if the USA government survive or perish. Over a span of eighty years as the USA government slowly grew into this monster size welfare state it was also taking on and carrying mountain size financial-burdens.

Every financial-burden the government gladly takes on cost money, but, the sad fact is the government has no money of its own. The government can do the talk but guess who is going to do the walk.

That mean every financial-burden the government takes on will be paid out of the profit margin of business people, because there won't be any wages paid to employees to tax unless the business first make a profit.

And as the government takes more and more profit fewer and fewer businesses will have enough profit left to survive on, let alone hire more workers.

The fact is the financial-burdens placed on the backs of USA business people cannot be carried much longer, the begging and borrowing has played out. Now, like bees in a hive the queen must be saved at all cost, we the people must save our USA government at all cost.

Never mind the learned experts, at this late stage there is only one way the USA government can be saved, especially with our freedom intact. The USA government must be reset back to default like the founding fathers designed it, There is no other way to save the USA government and the industrialized world.

That mean except for funding only community wise shelters, kitchens, and medical clinics the government shall be limited to defending the nation both internally and externally and doing only the bare necessary things the people can't do for themselves.

All other obligations shall be jettisoned to the private sector through privatization.

Otherwise, the financial-burdens now being carried by big government will soon leave no profit margin for USA private businesses to survive on, which is still the true economically engine for the entire world economy.

That is the only way to save the USA government with our freedom intact because the global economy is going to collapse sooner than we think. If everything else fails we will still have a lean but mean USA government intact to save the industrialized world. The financial-burdens must be jettisoned or nothing will be saved so help me GOD.

You can squeeze a lemon only so many times before there is no juice left, that is a law of nature. The only way to keep our welfare state afloat is to make millions upon millions of Americans debt slaves, while others freeload. It is already happening but it is going to get a lot worse.

FUTURE USA BLUEPRINT
FREDDIE L. SIRMANS, SR'S LOG: 11 JUNE 2009, 1828 HOURS LATE ENTRY:
On our welfare state beast's march to seize absolute power there is only one safeguard

left to prevent its complete consolidation. That last safeguard is the U.S. Congress. As for now the U.S. Congress still has control over this nations purse strings.

That is if they act now or very soon they can still cut taxes across the board to the bone. That is going to be the only thing that will starve this beast and stop it in its tracts. That is going to be the only thing that will prevent a complete take over of private business and absolute control.

However, I can assure you if Congress dilly dally too long they will end up as just a group of ceremonial figure heads. And our welfare state beast will have consolidated its power. Light, lights, lights, the movie is over folks, that was the wild imagination of this neurotic writer.

Nothing I just wrote is to be taken serious as real or fact. Thank God I didn't let my imagination get too carried away. Stay tuned for future episodes.

PS: In a family or in a nation whoever is the provider is the boss, in a free society the government should be a dependent of the people, not the people a dependent of the government. Only cutting taxes to the bone across the board will put the people back in control. However, don't bet the farm on it.

FREDDIE L. SIRMANS, SR'S LOG: 10 JUNE 2009, 1220 HOURS FUTURE USA BLUEPRINT

Here I go again giving an imaginary analysis that I dreamed up with no real life information to back me up. As I sit back in my recliner and watch the way our liberal welfare state beast is grabbing power and flexing its muscles I am almost in awe of its raw display of power. Or course I am one hundred and eighty degrees opposed to what is taking place.

I too believe the USA economy is headed toward a collapse, but I believe the best way to save our freedom and country is through mass tax cuts across the board. And get government completely out of the market place then deflation and the free market place will save this great country with our freedom intact.

I believe the great thinkers along with the movers and shakers within the power structure of this country know that the USA economy is on its last lap. I think the million dollar question was can the USA survive an economic collapse as a free market place nation, or should the government have total control over everything.

I think they have decided the government must seize total control over private business and everything else. I think the "Blueprint" is the government must have absolute junta like power for the USA to survive an economic collapse. Lord God I beg in your name, save our great nation.

IS THE USA DUMB, STUPID, OR JUST PLAIN NAIVE?
FREDDIE L. SIRMANS, SR'S LOG: 04 JUNE 2009, 1748 HOURS
IS THE USA DUMB, STUPID, OR JUST PLAIN NAIVE?
We have all of our survival eggs in one basket; I think that is dumb, stupid, or just plain naive. No matter what name you may call me it won't prove me wrong. Freedom in the USA will soon be over if good men of wisdom continue to say nothing.

Like a broken record as long as I have the freedom to I'm going to stay stuck on shouting to all who will listen that the USA must cut taxes to the bone across the board. I believe there is no way freedom can survive very much longer in the USA unless taxes are cut to the bone across the board.

I base this on a lack of good judgment and wisdom because our welfare state has destroyed good judgment in 95 percent of the American voters. No government with a strong survival instinct and proper judgment would allow all of its survival eggs to be in just one basket.

Good men took the course of least resistance and allowed a "New Deal' baby to slowly grow and take away our nations independent frontier like spirit. Now, with our welfare state beast planted firmly in control as a social and nuclear family provider there is very little power the average Joe/Jane has except to vote.

And that is practically worthless, because he lacks the judgment to vote for what is in the long term best interest of his country in my opinion. Today the survival of over 300 million Americans are in only one basket our sugar daddy welfare state provider, and when it collapses there won't be any order, except out of the barrel of a gun.

There will never be enough tax dollars to ever satisfy our welfare states appetite. That means it is only a matter of time before our welfare state tax bleeds us to death. When that happens it will mean millions upon millions of dependent Americans are going to be left physical and culturally unprepared for survival.

That is why no matter what they call me as long as I have breath in my body I'm going to continue to plead, yell, turn flips, or whatever to stress the dangers of not rebuilding our nuclear and extended family system, even if no one ever listens. The following No's used to be three additional egg baskets, but not anymore.

We have almost no strong nuclear and extended family system left, especially among African Americans. We have almost no strong moral and family values left, a kid can hardly use a computer without being exposed to smut. We have no adequate emergency bartering capacity with small farmers and home gardeners left to give this nation time to save our freedom if a calamity strikes.

Instead good men for years has stood by and let the shallow minded liberals slowly destroy this great nation with this welfare state. Sure, if taxes were cut to the bone across the board it will cause much, much hardship and suffering, but it will give this great nation a fighting chance to survive with our freedom intact.

Otherwise, we can sell the last of our soul and pride and this welfare state is still going to collapse. If we don't act first and Mother Nature has to steps in herself to enforce its natural selection law we will have no control and that could mean back to the Stone Age.

One positive, is a tax cut to the bone across the board will reset government back to default which is the way the founding fathers designed it to be. The USA government was never designed to be a social and nuclear family provider.

The USA government was designed to protect the nation from both internal and external threats, and do only the bare necessary things the citizens couldn't do for themselves. However, since the welfare state has made millions upon millions of citizens solely dependent on the government for survival they can never be abandoned.

Therefore, added to governments responsibility to protect the nation from internal and external threats, it now has an additional duty to provide community shelters, kitchens, and medical clinics, but very little else. The reason for little else is the Nuclear and extended family must be rebuilt at all cost and that can never happen unless there is a survival need for it.

A woman must have a survival need for a man, and a man must have a survival need for a woman for any society to survive long term. With the government out of private business and out of the way, then like a Phoenix rising up out of the ashes private enterprise with entrepreneurs will save our great country with our freedom intact.

On the other hand, to continue down the doomsday road we are on by trying to keep tax feeding our welfare state beast we are going to end up losing our freedom our country and everything else when this beast finish taxing us to death.

Like I've said before our welfare state is going to soon fall from its own weight because with the printing presses humming 24-7 it still won't be enough to keep this ferocious tax eating beast fed. Our greatest threat is to keep masses of people from starving, but never under estimate the American spirit. The old American frontier spirit is not all dead, yet.

We will survive. Excuse me for getting a little long winded. Thank you God for my life, health, and strength.....

FREDDIE L. SIRMANS, SR'S DOOMSDAY LOG BOOK

FREDDIE L. SIRMANS, SR'S LOG: 03 JUNE 2009, 1025 HOURS.

LATE ENTRY

It is a fact the higher all taxes across the board the fewer and fewer businesses are going to make a profit. It is not just me saying it; it is nature's law of natural selection in action. The liberals have been willing to beg, borrow, and steal to feed and support the appetite of our monster size welfare state beast.

We have sold down the river our soul, our manufacturing base, and just about everything else all to support this liberal created welfare state beast. Now, almost like a junkie on the streets, there is nothing we won't do to get this beast his fix.

Most people that read my writing see me as a lowly pest that can be swatted away anytime, but the liberals know better. The liberals see me as a real threat to their God and master, the welfare state beast. The reason is because I am coming in under the radar and landing some small but deadly strategic blows.

God I ask in your name, save our great nation.

FREDDIE L. SIRMANS, SR'S LOG: 01 JUNE 2009, 1910 HOURS LECTURE #4 ON THE UNITED STATES ECONOMY

As a lone writer let me say up front I don't expect many people to agree with me on hardly anything I write. In fact even myself, I hope I'm wrong about most of the things I write about. Sure, some people think I'm an idiot stuck on stupid because like a broken record I keep repeating across the board cut taxes to the bone, cut taxes to the bone.

I don't just believe it I know it for a fact that our freedom and economy will never be save unless taxes is cut to the bone. I also know that the law of natural selection is going to make it impossible to prevent the United States economy from collapsing unless taxes are cut to the bone.

I believe the whole USA economy is out of balanced and top heavy with too high taxes already. I believe all of the actions our management economists is doing is just buying time and holding on to the fantasy that we can keep paying for this monster size welfare state that is sucking the freedom and life blood out of this great nation.

I'm able to look past all of the fog and distractions and bore right to the heart of our economic problem. Now, forget about all of this other nonsense and focus on the thing that really matters, and that is profit, profit, and more profit if you want a successful free market place.

It all starts with a profit and unless a nation has masses upon masses of business people making a profits the government ain't gonna have nothing to tax. A successful free market place economy is the only economical system that can feed all of its people and more.

No other system even comes close. I'm going to clue you in on something right now, mass starving and hunger will be coming our way, it always does, you just wait until our welfare state beast finish destroying our private businesses and our free market place.

Yes, printing all of this worthless money is insane, but the thing that caused all of this sky is the limit inflation that is killing us is from government giving out free money on an individual basis. Doing that subsides price rising and allows merchants to keep raising the cost of living on everyone.

If not for that it would be impossible for prices or the cost of living to go higher than the masses of poor could pay out of pocket. And believe it or not the poor and the nation would be far better off today. Without government giving out money on an individual basis the poor would quickly rebuild the nuclear family to survive like all throughout history.

Worldwide the welfare state nations has left ninety five percent of its people too shallow with weak survival instincts to know that we can't survive as civilized societies when the global economy soon collapses. The free individual hand out act not only inflated our currency out of sight, it destroyed the need to depend on the nuclear family.

Now, if we lose our job half of us will end up homeless. I close for now, I don't want to get too long winded, stay tuned for the next episode.

NEW TRAIL BLAZING BREAKTHROUGH WEIGHT LOSING BATTLE!
This weight control program I have just developed is truly a break through;

because for the first time in my life of 68 years I feel I have dominant control over my compulsive overeating.

Anyone familiar with my writing knows that I have a super strong belief in "positive thinking" to change behavior. To those that don't know what positive thinking is, I will explain.

It is a technique to change behavior; take a phrase or quote and repeats it over and over to yourself. It doesn't need to be repeated aloud.

However, to be effective it must be repeated at least fifty or more times every day. The more times it is repeated the faster it will work because it is the repeating process itself that breaks through to the subconscious.

The quote to repeat is: I can keep small all of my food portions, (through God which strengthens me)." The through God part can be left out or changed to fit ones own deity if desired. It may take as long as a year or longer to fully kick in, and bear fruit, but if one doesn't quit the repeating process is guaranteed to get results.

Just keep repeating the quote to yourself at

least 50 times or more every day, and never quit until your goal is reached. God will make a way out of no way. Mighty forces will come to your aid. It will work if one doesn't quit.

A word of advice about changing eating behavior, it can be done but it is not a simple or easy matter. The only guarantee is to never stop repeating the quote because fat cells don't like being starved. One may start craving sweets and wanting to eat everything in sight and feeling the quote is a waste of time all to get you to quit repeating the quote.

The body cells in cahoots with the mind will play all kinds of tricks to get you to quit but in the end you will reach your goal if you stay with it and never quit. It is like breaking in a wild horse.

The wild horse is going to buck and try everything in its power to throw you off but if you can hang on and ride it out you will obtain your goal. The reason it is so hard to lose weight is your body cells in cahoots with your mind will use reward and punishment against you.

The punishment of hunger may seem much more severe. And at the same time the good taste of food may seem much more rewarding. However, in the end the mind must try to carry out any image constantly presented to it.

WEIGHT BATTLE BEGINS!
I, Freddie L. Sirmans, Sr. have decided to share with my readers the inner working of my mind out loud as I try to discover secrets on how to lose weight.

The tactics I try may not work; still, I decided to share with my readers as I plot my strategy on defeating my sometimes overpowering compulsive overeating habit.

WARNING: I check with my doctor before trying anything new or stressful.

The previous positive thinking quote with enough time is effective, but, I've decided to create this newer untested quote developed by me anyway. I don't fully recommend it yet because it may cause some stress. And anyone that uses it does it at their own risk.

Positive thinking has been proven to change behavior when the same quote or phrase is repeated to oneself at least 50 times or more every day. The more times it is repeated the faster it works. The quote to repeat, which I don't recommend yet is to just say over and over: **"Eating too much food is dangerous."**

Positive thinking is a slow process, sometimes it can take 6 months to a year or even longer to fully kick in.

Just as our main survival responses are fight or flight, reward or punishment are the main responses that control our behavior. Nothing in nature is all good or all bad; it is a matter of degree and balance.

The reward of pleasure and good taste is necessary to make sure we eat, but, the balance arm of too much is not kicking in with compulsive over eaters like me.

So, maybe through "Positive thinking" an artificial overriding braking system will work. There is nothing to lose but weight.

The problem of overeating starts from eating when not hungry for whatever reason. Once the "Don't eat when not hungry" response is shoved completely out of the picture, for some, overeating becomes a compulsion.

Then any attempt to limit the amount and push away from the table is looked upon as a cruel punishment and taking away a deserved reward.

The key is to realize that too much food intake is really a punishment of survival instead of just a harmless too much of a good thing reward.

10 NOVEMBER 2010, 1853 HOURS: Last entry.

19 NOVEMBER 2010, 1708 HOURS: New Progress report in my quest to discover secrets on losing weight I will use the "Positive thinking" technique on myself to gauge my progress.

From my previous entry I established that it is reward or punishment that controls all normal human behavior. Also, I established that once the "Don't eat when not hungry" response is ignored enough the inner mind then see all eating including over eating as a reward. Then no amount of eating is viewed as punishment and stomach capacity becomes the only stopping point.

Now, the first strategy I'm going to use is to set eating rules followed by punishment for every infraction of those rules.

Rule number one: I'm going to decide on what weight I plan to get down to and list it on paper. My current weight is

252LBS and my goal weight is 195LBS.

Rule number two: I'm going to limit all meals to one helping, no second for anything. I try to make it a habit to bless the food before each meal, that signals the start of the meal and after that no seconds. Then nothing else can be added.

Rule number three: Set everything I plan to eat before me before I start, after that no going back for seconds. Once I start eating and notice something I really like and want, I'll just remember I can have it my next meal 4 hours later.

Rule number four: No snacking between meals.

Rule number five: No meals will be eaten at less than four hour intervals. All rules and conditions may be waived if I'm sick or doing extra strenuous work.

Rule number six: Unlimited amounts of water are permitted at all times, but Juices, sodas, or high protein drinks are permitted only at four hours intervals

Snacking is something that needs to be discouraged. Contrary to what people

think most people are not overweight because of extra large over powering meals, but because of snacking on junk foods and sweets, especially kids.

* Allow for an occasional glass of wine

Remember reward or punishment is what shapes all behavior and that includes eating behavior. So, that means if I break one of my own eating rules I must punish myself for the infraction.

Whoa, hold on, I'm not talking about any harsh, cruel, or diabolical like punishment, but still, a message must be sent that rule breaking will not be tolerated.

The punishment stick I'm going to use on myself is going to be the punishment of fasting limited to juices, sodas, high protein drinks, or water but absolutely no food.

All punishment will be limited to a minimum of 4 hours up to a maximum of 24 hours. I'm going to assign a set punishment for certain infractions for now and may add more later.

SET PUNISHMENTS:
(1.) Punishment for all rule violations except snacking: 24 hours of fasting limited to juices, sodas, or high protein

drinks at not less than 4 hour intervals. I can drink water anytime, but absolutely no food for 24 hours.

(2.) Punishment for breaking the "No snacking" rule: 4 hours of fasting limited to water only but absolutely no food.

Here is the skinny on enforcing punishment for rule violations: This is something that must be enforced or else abandon this whole thing right now. That is because I have challenged my inner mind for dominance over my compulsive overeating habit and if I don't follow through with enforcement; my inner mind will come roaring back with a vengeance.

This is something I must never; never start or it will end up punishing me with much more extra weight gain unless I'm prepared to follow through on my punishment rules. My inner compulsions will reassert its dominance and take revenge if I become weak and fail to enforce all of the rules I set out. I hope you get the picture, messing around with something like this is not for the weak and goodie, goodie two shoes type, this is all about dominating or being dominated.

I may start craving sweet and wanting to eat everything in sight and end up gaining weight and eating far more than ever. That is why any serious major change in behavior is always going to cause some temporary stress.

I've decided to start repeating my latest **"Eating too much food is dangerous"** positive thinking quote. Also, you keep checking I plan to make at least monthly progress reports.
19 NOVEMBER 2010, 2130 HOURS: Last entry

21 NOVEMBER 2010, 2025 HOURS: New progress report.
Unlimited amounts of water are permitted at all times but juices, sodas, and high protein drinks are permitted only at four hour intervals.

There is no restriction on the amount of juices, sodas, or protein drink consumed at a time. Also, there is no set amount of meals per day, but no meal or drink is permitted to be served less than 4 hour intervals.

WARNING NOTE: Remember, I have the right and power to set or change the rules anytime I want to, but, by God whatever rules that I list on paper must be obeyed and enforce to the tee or I suffer the consequences.

If I'm not willing to punish myself for every rule infractions I must abandon this program this minute otherwise my inner mind is going to get revenge on me with much, much more weight gain for challenging it in the first place.

WEIGHT PROGRESS REPORT: Goal weight 195LBS
MONTH---YEAR--STARTED Wt.----CURRENT WT.
November 2010---252Lbs----------250LBS
December 2010--------------------247LBS
January 2011------------------------245LBS
February 2011----------------------244LBS
March 2011-------------------------
April 2011--------------------------
May 2011---------------------------
June 2011--------------------------
July 2011--------------------------
August 2011----------------------
September 2011------------------
October 2011--------------------
November 2011------------------
December 2011------------------
29 NOVEMBER 2010, 1045 HOURS: Last entry.

I'M ONE THAT SUFFERS FROM DIABETES!

So, I decided to write the very basics of understanding diabetes. They call it sugar diabetes and the old folks used to just say he/she "Got sugar." However, that is true, but, that kind of talk can be misleading and doesn't tell the whole story.

The real story is carbohydrates are what determine the level of sugar in the blood, not just sugar and sweets. Yet, most people still automatically think of just sugar and sweets as the big bad boogie man that must be avoided at all cost.

The fact is sugar or sweets are only one type of carbohydrate. Things like bread, pasta, fruit, and vegetables are all carbohydrates that turns into sugar for the body to use for energy. Also, another big factor that determines blood sugar levels is the speed at which a carbohydrate turns into sugar.

Some carbohydrates turns into sugar very rapid and others very slow. The pancreas produces insulin to keep too much sugar from getting into the blood, but a diabetic person doesn't produce enough insulin or fast enough to block rapid sugar producing carbohydrates, thereby allowing too much sugar to overflow into the blood stream. However, a diabetic can do a lot through diet to control blood sugar level by eating carbohydrates that turns into sugar very slowly like green beans, broccoli, and leafy vegetables. That way his lesser producing pancreas may be able to keep up and keep his blood sugar level within the normal range.

The diet first method along with taking the mineral chromium picolinate may work for some, but, never try any method without first checking with a doctor and having a home testing kit to monitor ones own blood sugar level at all times.

For us to live our bodies must get energy from the foods we eat. Our bodies breaks down the foods we eat in three ways, they are carbohydrates, proteins, and fats. Proteins and fats alone don't turn into sugar or raise blood sugar levels as long as no gravies, sauces, or anything else is included. In fact some carbohydrates are high in proteins such as beans and nuts.

But, for some unexplained reason fats tends to hinder blood sugar levels from dropping from whatever level it is at the time, Otherwise without fats it tends to drop like a rock.

The body prefers and will always choose the sugar from carbohydrates first to get its needed energy, then as second choice it will turns to proteins for energy.

NOTE: I am not a trained health care professional in anyway, but with my limited knowledge I decided to write this article anyway, I can only hope that I have been helpful to someone in someway. God bless you all.

SIRMANS LOG: 3 DECEMBER 2010, 1841 HOURS.

LESS STRESS MORE SUCCESS WITH THIS PRAYER
A PRAYER GUARANTEED FOR LESS STRESS AND MORE SUCCESS!!!

To my father who is in heaven I will strive to always serve you first. I will strive to treat all people well as I would like to be treated. I will strive to wish all people goodwill even when it is not returned. I will strive to repeat this prayer twice a day for as long as I live. I thank you God for my life health and strength and for what I do have here on earth. I can face and do all things through you my God. Amen.

This prayer was created by self-made writer Freddie L. Sirmans, Sr. mainly to aid the African American people but it is for anyone that finds it useful. Because of so much violent infighting within the African American community he felt the need to create this prayer.

Mr. Sirmans knows this prayer works and in six months will rid much of the negative thinking and myth's that holds so many back and keeps them down.

proof of a pudding is in the taste, proof of this prayer is your stress level and positive outlook after saying it a while. This prayer is not limited to just my own belief one can make a substitution and use their own deity.
.

I will guarantee you that anyone who says this prayer twice a day for 6 months will be healed or ninety percent improved. It won't matter if its stress or any other condition a new positive outlook and change will take place. However, you will never find out if you don't test it for yourself.

POST STATEMENT (PS :) I, Freddie L. Sirmans, Sr. gives my direct permission to whom ever it may concern that he/she can copy this prayer and promote it anyway he/she see fit providing not a single word is changed.

Signed: Freddie L. Sirmans on this 14th day

of February two thousand ten (2010).

GREAT HEALING QUOTES

As a young child being punished as a bed wetter caused me to have neurotic symptoms for as long as I can remember. Today I'm over sixty seven years of age and for the last forty years I've used positive thinking as a tool to try to solve the riddle of my neurotic symptoms. And after all of these years I've come to one conclusion, you can't solve the riddle, but, you can face it down. Another thing I've learned is the real hidden enemy is "unforgiveness."

It makes some turn on themselves and self-destruct. It makes some turn on others and cause great destruction to others. My offer of help to others battling and struggling with this hidden enemy is: There is hope and relief if you are willing to learn forgiveness. Not everyone wants to learn forgiveness. I feel blessed and thankful that all of my effort over the years has not been wasted.

I have developed more than one positive thinking quote over the years, but I believe this one is my "Holy Grail." As always, the positive thinking technique is to take a quote and repeat it to yourself over and over at a minimum of fifty times a day. It helps to repeat it more because the more it is repeated the faster it works. It is not enough to believe and know it works; the repeating process itself is what breaks through to the subconscious.

My life long guaranteed Holy Grail positive thinking quote is: "I can face and forgive all things,"(optional) through God who strengthens me.

CONCERNING TOURETTE SYNDROME AND OTHER PHOBIA'S:

I saw a program on TV the other day on Tourette syndrome and it made me think that disease over in my mind. The first thing in my view is instead of people taking all of these mind altering drug with side effects, I believe my "Holy grail" positive thinking quote offers a superior natural remedy. The working of the mind deals only in images and it doesn't distinguish between a good image or a bad image; it just obeys the strongest command image presented.

The reason may be an unloving environment or any threat to ones survival that causes an emotion to stamp a survival image on ones mind against the will of a weaken ego. The natural reaction of the ego is to resist any unacceptable image, which can be counterproductive, because that is what stamps the unwanted image on the subconscious mind. Therefore, the harder one tries to mentally resist any emotional image the more strongly the image becomes and the mind will obey the strongest command image.

Example:
The more one fears he is going to do or say something shocking the more likely that fear will over power his ego and make it happen.
Decoded:
Fear actually means lack of emotional resistance energy and the more one fears he is going to lose, the harder the mind tries to obey the command image to lose. That is why animals can smell fear and go in for an easy kill. Remember, the emotions are super powerful images, but they can never defeat the ego if the ego calls their bluff. No emotion can force the ego to do anything that it really doesn't want to do.

In childhood when a child is under grave mental or physical threats and abuse the mind will go to extreme lengths to instill emotional images to assure survival under adverse conditions. Another example: We all have heard the term "Animal magnetism or something chemical." Well, in my view, super powerful emotional sexual energy like that comes from some form of childhood sexual abuse.

I haven't studied psychology or anything of the sort, but I have enough common sense to know that things like sexual obsession and sexual projections have to do with childhood sexual abuse. Just count yourself lucky if you have never had to escape from someone abused and cursed with this energy. Once involved for some reason it is extremely hard to get someone like that out of your mind because of their primitive enticing sexual power.

They have the ability to turn one on to a super sexual charged level. Also, most people cursed with this energy tend to be abusers themselves. Because of the power of the mind a molester may start off being in control, but the table can get flipped on him, that is why some accuse their victim of being possessed.

So, when you see a previously well controlled individual completely fall apart in a new relationship, don't be so quick to condemn. There are energy forces out there that only a super strong moral person can resist. When these victims are back in a normal environment without any threats those same powerful emotional images may still be protecting them the same way making them seem weird and abnormal in close contact.

Now, my solution is to deal with the situation in a tandem way. Like I said, the emotions have no real power, except to bluff and put up a facade. So, when confronted by overpowering self-guilt and self-shame all one has to do is call their bluff by facing them head on and in short order they will start fading away, that makes "Facing" the keyword. Now, to the other side of the tandem. To instill a strong healthy ego in a child it is so important for that child to have at least some love and acceptance.

Otherwise, the emotions of fear, shame, and guilt can leave the child vulnerable to all sorts of mental illnesses. There is a world of difference between being the way one wants to be and being the way one really is. So, if one has self images he can't accept for whatever reason, no amount of wishful thinking is going to change that fact. When the ego hates the way one is, the emotions of self-shame and self-guilt can make one feel worthless and unworthy.

Self-shame, self-guilt, and self-hate can destroy the mental self (ego) the same as if someone physical blows one's brains out. In this case, "Forgiveness" is the keyword. Therefore, my positive thinking natural remedy is: "I can face and forgive all things (optional) through God who strengthens me." "I can face and forgive all things." "I can face and forgive all things......

Forgiveness
1. It is the only thing that will ease embedded anger and hate.
2. If one has been hurt and mistreated, especially by a friend or loved one, forgiveness may be the only thing that will ease ones raging anger and desire to reject, avenge, destruct, or destroy.
3. There are no greater powers on earth than love and forgiveness.
4. There is no mental condition or problem that love and forgiveness can't heal.
5. Nothing can mental defeat one that can genuine love and forgive.
6. You can't change other people but other people will respond to a change in you.
7. It's a proven fact that the power of positive thinking can change behavior.
8. To acquire genuine joy and happiness it is one of the best tools, but only the truly unselfish will forgive no matter how they are treated in return.
9. To acquire this awesome power, repeat to yourself fifty or more times a day the following "world's most powerful healing quote" whenever and as long as necessary.

10. **THE WORLD'S MOST POWERFUL HEALING QUOTE IS:**

"I can wish all people goodwill no matter how they treat me." Note: To be effective one should never repeat more than one quote at a time during a six month period.

11. Actually wishing all people goodwill even if its not returned is not to please others, but to mentally and emotionally guarantee a bright future for yourself. It is still true that "Attitude determine altitude." You are how you treat all people including those you have power over when no one else is around. So, if you remain a loving, caring, and forgiving person you will reap those rewards in life.

Note:

Forgiveness does not mean that one tolerates abuse or mistreatment in any way. You separate yourself from any abusive situation, then forgive and move on. As a rule the choices we make determines our fate. But, self preservation should always come first.

MR. SIRMANS VIEW ON CHRISTIANITY:

Mr. Sirmans for one doesn't believe modern civilization would be where it is today without Christianity. He thinks the main ingredient in Christianity that allows it to advance civilization more than any other religion is its emphasis on forgiveness, and the "Sermon on the mount" message.

It may not seem like much, but without the power of forgiveness, foreign and domestically everyone could still be emphasizing tit for tat, eye for eye, tooth for tooth, regressing back to the Stone Age. That is what some countries would do if left entirely to themselves. Lastly, I must include a count your bless quote as a stress reliever because of so many people on legal mind altering drugs.

True joy and happiness is determine by how one accepts and appreciate life, not what one have or may not have. The old biblical advice is still true today as it was five thousand years ago. Remember to count your blessings, or never forget to count your blessings. As always the power in positive thinking is in the repeating process itself. Whenever one is feeling down and stressed out, repeat this quote over and over to yourself, "Thank you God for my life, health, and strength, thank you, thank you....

Another good positive quote to repeat to yourself when you just can't seem to make ends meet is, " Thank you God for what I do have, Thank you, thank you...Say it as much and as long as necessary until the storm passes over. This is from the horse's mouth itself. Over the years I've used this quote to get over my darkest hours. There have been times when I've felt totally unlovable with no hope to ever find happiness.

All I knew to do was put one foot in front of the other and go through the motion of living. But, deep down in my soul there was always an unwavering fighting instinct to survive. So far back I can't even remember I instinct knew that if one can refuse to hate he cannot be mentally destroyed. I knew that as long as one can genuine love and forgive someway somehow he would triumph in the end.

You will never see those that can genuine love and forgive in mental wards and stressed out loser with no hope. Enough said, thank you for taking the time to read my work.

WORLD GREATEST STRESS RELIEVING AND HEALING QUOTE EVER CONCEIVED BY MAN!

QUOTE: **I can wish all people goodwill through God which strengthens me.** One can leave off the through God which strengthens me or substitute in place of God ones own deity. Just repeat the quote to yourself as many times as necessary or until the storm passes over. No one else has to know what you are repeating to yourself.

I promise you if you have trouble on your job, in your marriage, or whatever, your stress will vanish, it is not a cure all, but, a stress free healing process will began. True joy and happiness comes from within. But, you can't find it from within. You find it by caring, helping, and serving others!

THE END

Freddie L. Sirmans, Sr.
Valdosta, Georgia USA
Website: FLSirmans.com